Tan Huaixiang

character costume figure drawing

Step-by-Step Drawing Methods for Theatre Costume Designers

AMSTERDAM • BOSTON • HEIDELBERG • LONDON • NEW YORK • OXFORD
PARIS • SAN DIEGO • SAN FRANCISCO • SINGAPORE • SYDNEY • TOKYO

Focal Press is an imprint of Elsevier

ELSEVIER

Focal Press

Focal Press is an imprint of Elsevier
200 Wheeler Road, Burlington, MA 01803, USA
Linacre House, Jordan Hill, Oxford OX2 8DP, UK

Library of Congress Cataloging-in-Publication Data
Tan, Huaixiang.
  Character costume figure drawing : step-by-step drawing methods for
theatre costume designers / by Tan Huaixiang.
     p. cm.
Includes index.
  ISBN-13: 978-0-240-80534-4
  ISBN-10: 0-240-80534-8

  1. Costume. 2. Costume design. 3. Drawing–Technique. I. Title.
  PN2067.T36 2004
  792.02'6–dc22

                                   2003023767

British Library Cataloguing-in-Publication Data
A catalogue record for this book is available from the British Library.

For information on all Focal Press publications
visit our website at www.focalpress.com

05 06 07 08 10 11   9 8 7 6 5 4 3 2

Printed in China

Table of Contents

Credits to Walt Stanchfield: **Words of Wisdom**
A handout for people who are interested in animation drawings or want to be animators.

Preface

As an instructor, I have been working with theatre costume design students for many years.
I know how students become frustrated
when drawing human figures, and I understand their
needs. I feel I have a responsibility to write this book
in order to help students who have trouble drawing,
and hope this book will greatly help all prospective
designers out there. Because English is my second
language, writing this book has been a very difficult
task. Some days I felt it was impossible and wanted
to give up. But the desire to help my students—fu-
ture designers—encouraged me to continue.

The development of this book is based on years
of experience with educational theatre and, more
specifically, my teaching experience with college students. I know they need a guide they can use in their
free time to educate themselves and practice figure
drawing to become skilled costume designers. I tried
to make this book instructional and fundamental. I
tried to keep it simple, direct, and straightforward. It
is difficult for me to express myself exactly the way I
want to in English, so I hope the visual images speak
for themselves. The various illustrations demonstrate my step-by-step processes. I have incorporated
a number of examples of my costume designs into
each subject to give more visual explanations on the
topic and to show how to utilize line quality, form,
and texture to create facial expressions and body
language, and to explore variations in characters and
garments. I have tried hard to make this book easily
comprehensible and easy to follow. I hope this book
is both useful to students and entertaining to casual
readers. It can be used as a reminder or as inspira-
tion by college students and professionals who are interested in character drawings for all different types
of character creations. I hope this book will help
costume design students enjoy the process of figure
drawing, and if it helps even a little with design artwork, I will feel rewarded.

Acknowledgments

I would like to thank all the professionals and friends who encouraged me to write this book.

A special thanks to Bonnie J. Kruger, who introduced me to the Focal Press. Thank you to the Focal Press for your support and understanding.

Thanks to all my professors at the Central Academy of Drama in Beijing, China: Hou Qidi, Ma Chi, Xing Dalun, Wang Ren, Li Chang, Zhang Bingyao, Qi Mudong, Zhang Chongqing, He Yunlan, Yie Ming, An Lin, Wang Xiping, Sun Mu, and Li Dequan. You laid the foundation for me to pursue and achieve what I have today. You nurtured and motivated me to start my theatre design career. Your influence has changed my life.

Thanks to the professors in the Department of Theatre Arts at Utah State University, Colin B. Johnson, Sid Perkes, and Bruce E. McInroy, for your kindness, advice, and support. You taught me how to survive in the United States and were patient and understanding at all times. I greatly treasure your instruction.

Thanks to all my former chairmen with whom I worked: Sid Perks, Bruce A. Levitt, Wesley Van Tassel, and Donald Seay. Thank you for being wonderful, understanding leaders and for teaching me discipline and timeliness. Your positivity will always be remembered.

Thanks to the UCF Faculty Center for Teaching and Learning computer lab professors and staff for all your great help whenever I needed it for my classes and computer problems.

Thanks to the entire faculty and staff in the department of theatre at the University of Central Florida for all your help, support, and kindness.

Thanks to my dear friends Xiangyun Jie, Julia Zheng, Helen Huang, Peiran Teng, Dunsi Dai, Liming Tang, HaiBou Yu, Zhang Chongqing, and Rujun Wang for giving me unconditional support and advice. You put a smile on my face when I needed it most.

Thank you to my parents for shaping me into the person I am today. A big thank you goes to my daughter, Yingtao Zhang, for all your inspirational ideas and unending support and encouragement. Thanks to my husband, Juli Zhang, for encouraging me and helping me to succeed in my own professional life.

Finally, thank you to all my students for your tolerance and for allowing me to be your instructor.

Introduction

This book is visually oriented to provide a simple, viewable guide that focuses on the principles and formats of character costume figure drawings. Throughout all the illustrations, you will see dimension and diversity in the characters. Facial expressions, body language, body action, and props are incorporated to clearly characterize each figure.

What Makes a Good Theatrical Costume Designer?

I would never say that a person who draws beautiful pictures is always a good costume designer. A good costume designer must have many other qualities and capabilities, such as imagination and knowledge in theatre, world history, theatre history, costume history, and literature. The designer must retain good communication and organizational skills; possess research and technical skills like drawing, rendering, computer graphics, costume construction, crafts, millinery, and personnel management; be a good team player; and even be in good health. All these factors make a wonderfully ideal costume designer. Drawing and painting skills are tools for helping a designer develop and express visual images and design concepts. Renderings are not the final product, the final product is the actual stage costume made suitable and proper for the actors.

The Importance of Personality and Body Language

To capture the impression of a character's spirit is always a goal when developing character figure drawings. By nature, we all relate to human emotion because we all experience it. Characters are human beings, and human beings all possess personalities. To portray a character's emotions and personality on paper is a challenge, but well worth the results. When I create costume designs, I try not only to illustrate the costumes, but also to portray a completed characterization. I try to manipulate every body part to build compositional beauty and artistically express the power of a character's substance. Every gesture, action, facial expression, and accessory will add meaning and entertainment to the design. People say that we should not judge a person by his or her appearance, but when an actor appears on stage, his or her appearance becomes significant. The character's body language reflects the soul and spirit of the character, and an interesting gesture helps to display the style of the costumes. Using body language to emphasize the personality and status of a character is to give the character an exciting appearance. Character figures enhance and adorn the costume designs, and they communicate with the director, actor, other designers, and the production team. Expressing the personality of the character in your drawings is like the saying, "A picture is worth a thousand words."

Philosophy for Drawing

Drawing human figures should be fun. Nobody was born an innate artist and nobody will become one overnight, but I believe that with some effort, anybody can draw. Although improving your drawing skills requires tremendous effort, enjoying it and being interested will greatly help. When you are driven to do well, you will. Watch, listen, and absorb.

To develop a more positive attitude, consider this: Just do it. Work helps. Avoid a pessimistic and sluggish attitude. Desire and dedication are the discipline of a career, and work is the language of that discipline.

POSITIVITY!

CONFIDENCE!

PRACTICE!

SUCCESS!

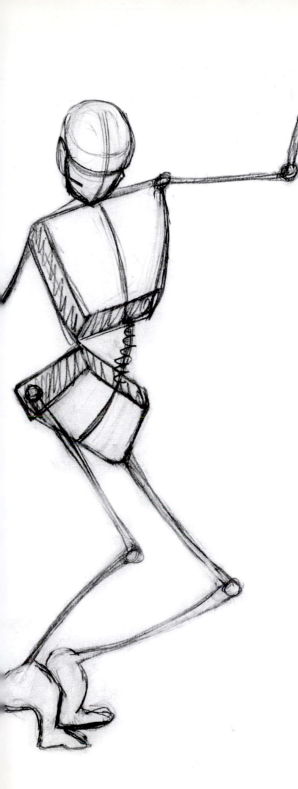

1

Drawing the Figure

My objective in writing this book is to show how to draw figures using a simple and easy drawing method. Specifically, the book is intended to help theatre students improve their drawing skills so that they can give effective design presentations. Most theatre students do not have any solid drawing training, nor do they have any human anatomy or figure-drawing courses in their curricula. Drawing requires a lot of practice and knowledge of the proportions of the human body. I believe that with effort, anybody can draw.

Theatre students typically have to do production assignments and work in the shops, helping to build either scenery or costumes for the production. Their time is occupied with those assignments, leaving them little time to improve their drawing skills. That is why I am trying to find a short, easy, and fast way to help them improve their drawing abilities. The methods in this book can be used without a model. However, if theatre students have the opportunity to draw the human figure from live models, they should do so. Drawing live models is a tremendous help in understanding the human body.

PROPORTIONS OF THE BODY

There are many concepts or methods for measuring the divisions of the human body. The eight-heads-tall figure proportion method is often used by artists or fashion illustrators. Some fashion drawings may use eight-and-a-half- or nine-heads-tall figures to demonstrate the garments, using a slim, sophisticated image. Realism is not intent of fashion designers or illustrators. Rather, their objective is to create a stylized or exaggerated version of reality, which today is a tall, slim, and athletic figure, with a long neck and long legs. Fashion illustrations emphasize the current ideals or trends of fashion beauty. The thin body and specific poses are designed to enhance the garments. Fashion illustrators are creating the images of fashionable products to stimulate customers to purchase the garments. Beautiful illustrations can impress and influence customers to buy and wear the advertised clothing.

Costume designs for theatrical productions are quite different from fashion illustrations. The costume designer uses the history of fashion as a reference for creating costumes for many varieties of characters or groups of characters in plays. The characters are everyday-life people: young or old, thin or heavy, short or tall, with different nationalities and particular personalities. Costume design for productions requires creating practical garments that are going to be worn on stage by believable characters who have well-defined personalities. Sometimes a well-defined character costume design can inspire the actors and enhance the design presentation for the production team. In my drawings and designs, I try to emphasize a realistic style of body proportions, but I use slightly exaggerated facial features and body language to create characters with personality. The real creative challenge is how to express personalities of characters.

Most of the proportions of the body that I used in this book are based on the theories of proportions used in many other art books. There are fantastic art books from which you can learn about the proportions of the body and about figure drawing techniques, such as *Bridgman's Complete Guide to Drawing from Life*, by George B. Bridgman; *The Complete Book of Fashion Illustration*, by Sharon Lee Tale and Mona Shafer Edwards; *The Human Figure: An Anatomy for Artists*, by David K. Rubins; *Drawing the Head and Figure*, by Jack Hamm; and *Drawing on the Right Side of the Brain*, by Betty Edwards. These books helped me improve my understanding of the human body and taught me how to present the body well. You can study the rules and principles of figure drawing but you have to learn how to use them through *practice*.

To give my characters a realistic appearance, I slightly change the size of the head. Compared to the eight-heads-tall proportions, I enlarge the head to extend outside the usual boundary of the first head area. This enlarges the head in proportion to the top half of the body. I keep the feet within the bottom-half portion of the body. When I start the foundation of a figure, however, I still start with the eight-heads-tall method because it is an even number and easier to divide for calculation purposes. My divisions on the body may differ from other books, but the measurements work for my figure drawings. My primary intent is to have a system that is easy to use.

The key for developing a character figure drawing that is in proportion is to keep the top half (from the crotch up to the top of the skull) equal to the bottom half (from the crotch down to the bottom of the feet). The crotch is the main division point. The head can actually be made either a little bigger or smaller. A small head will make the figure look taller or thinner; a bigger head will make the figure look shorter or chubbier. When keeping these measurements in mind, the figure will always look right.

I recommend that you use the following steps to create a figure drawing, until you become familiar with body proportions. Refer to Figures 1-1 and 1-2 as you complete these steps.

1. Place two marks on the paper — one on the top portion of the page, one on the bottom portion of the page — to indicate the height of the body. Then draw a vertical line from the top mark to the bottom mark. The composition of the figure should be considered; that is, keeping the figure centered or off-centered, more to the left or to the right side, and so on. These guidelines control the figure height.

2. Draw a mark at the middle point of the vertical line to find the middle point of the body. This mark is where the crotch is located and is also the half-height of the body. I am going to call the area from this mark up the upper half of the body. To me, this mark is the most critical reference point for good proportions of the body. (See Figure 1-1, mark #5.)

3. Divide the upper body from the top mark to the crotch line into four equal parts. This creates five marks but four portions. Number all the marks: The very top mark, mark #1, is the top of the skull; we won't use mark #2; mark #3 is the armpit; mark #4 is the waistline; and mark #5 is the half-body mark (it is also the crotch, pelvis, or hipline). The very bottom mark drawn in step 1 is mark #6. I will refer by numbers to these six marks extensively in the discussion that follows.

4. Make the head bigger compared to mark #2 (usually considered the chin in measurement

systems used in other drawing books). The head will be increased by adding a distance approximately the size of a chin from mark #2 down (see letter A on the sketch in Figure 1-1). This shortens the neck. Fashion drawings usually are just the opposite, showing a longer neck. The mark at letter A is going to be the bottom of the chin.

5. Draw an egg-shaped frame between the top mark and the chin mark, A, to indicate the shape of the head.

6. Divide the distance between mark #2 and the armpit line (mark #3) in half and mark it as letter B; this mark is going to be the shoulder line or collarbone. Generally speaking, the width of the shoulders is a measurement about two heads wide for females and two-and-a-half heads wide for males. Measure the width of the shoulders and add two marks (see letter C in Figure 1-1).

7. Divide the distance between mark #2 and the shoulder line, B, in half and add another mark. This mark helps to establish the shoulder-slope line (see letter D in Figure 1-1). Look at the sketch and review this in detail.

8. Divide the distance between the armpit (mark #3) and the waistline (mark #4) into four equal parts. Now you have drawn three marks to create four parts. The first mark from the top of this group is the bustline (see letter E in Figure 1-1); this mark usually refers to the nipples position or bustline. The third mark from the top is the bottom of the rib cage (see letter F in Figure 1-1). The second mark is not used.

9. Divide the distance between the waistline (mark #4) and the crotch or hipline (mark #5)

into four equal parts. The first mark is the top of the pelvis (see letter G in Figure 1-1). The male pelvis width is different from the female. The female hip width is usually wider than her shoulders. The male hip width is less wide than the shoulders. For both males and females, the width of the top of the pelvis

usually equals the width of the bottom of the rib cage or chest. The bottom of the pelvis/hipline/crotch line is wider than width of the the top of the pelvis (see letter H in Figure 1-1). The hipline's width will depend on whether you are drawing a female or male. The other two marks are not used.

1-1 Proportion of the Body, Marks A through H

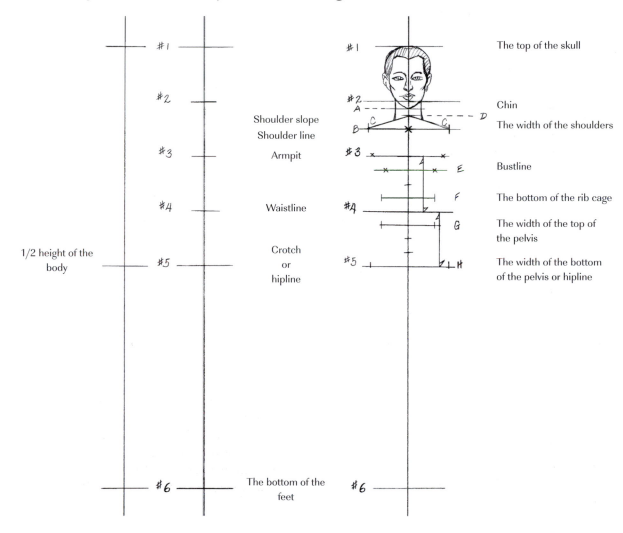

10. Treat the chest/rib cage as a tapered box (refer to Figure 1-2). Connect the shoulder line with the bottom of the rib cage to make a tapered-down box. The shoulder should be wider than the bottom of the rib cage. Keep both sides of the body symmetrical with the body centerline. The pit of the neck is at the middle of the shoulder line — it is the body centerline.

11. Treat the pelvis as a tapered-up box. Connect the top of the pelvis line with the bottom of the pelvis line (mark #5, also the hipline/crotch line) to draw a tapered-up box. The female hipline is wider than the male hipline.

12. The area from the crotch down will be for the legs and feet. The legs join the pelvis at the hipline. Before starting to draw the legs, divide the distance between mark #5 (crotch line) and mark #6 (the bottom of the feet) into four equal parts. Then mark them from the top down (see letters I, J, and K in Figure 1-2).

13. Divide the distance between K and mark #6 into three equal parts. The feet are drawn in the bottom third (see letter L in Figure 1-2).

14. Draw two lines from both corners of mark #5 (hipline/crotch) down to letter L to indicate the legs. Keep them symmetrical. Then divide these two lines in half; the middle marks on these two lines are the knee positions (see letter M in Figure 1-2). This method of drawing leg length avoids the leggy look of fashion-illustration figures. Our objective is to create a realistic look corresponding to the actors, rather than a fashion ideal.

15. The arms join to the chest at the shoulder line. In human anatomy theory, the upper arm from the shoulder to the elbow is longer than the distance from the elbow to wrist. In my method, I treat them as two equal parts in length for an easy calculation ratio. When the arm is hanging down, the elbow usually lines up with the waistline. The measurement from the shoulder to the elbow should equal the measurement from the elbow to the wrist. From the elbow joint, measure down to indicate the placement of the wrist.

16. Add hands to the wrists. The fingertips usually stop at letter I (the fifth head in other books). Asian people often have shorter arms, African people usually have longer arms, and Caucasians often have arms that are longer than Asians' but shorter than Africans'. There are many variations and exceptions to any racial generality.

1-2 Proportion of the Body, Marks I through M

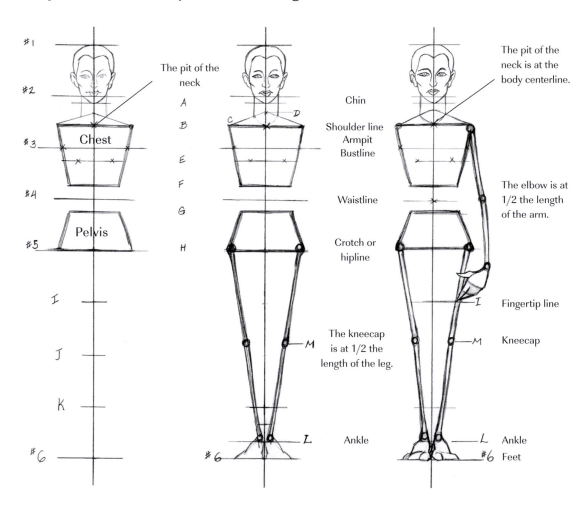

17. As shown in Figure 1-3, contour the body according to the basic bone/stick structure (see the section, "Contouring the Stick Figure"). Figures 1-4 and 1-5 show the contouring lines for the male and female body, respectively.

The proportions of the body, either seven- or eight-heads tall, work only for the body standing in a straight position. When the body is bending or the head is facing up or down, you cannot apply the measurements to the body because of foreshortening.

The body measurement methods used in this book are not the only methods you should follow, but I recommend you use my system as a guide or reference for drawing stage costumes.

1-3 Proportions of the Body, Stick Structure, Front and Back Views

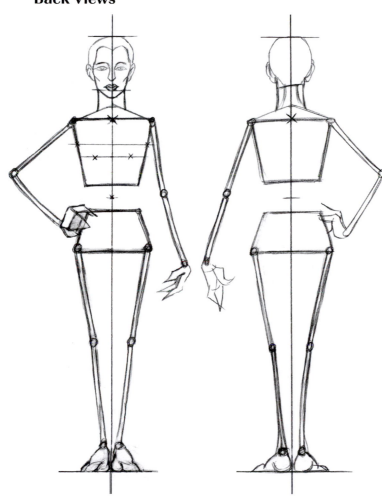

Front View   Back View

1-4 Contouring Lines for the Male Body, Front and Back Views

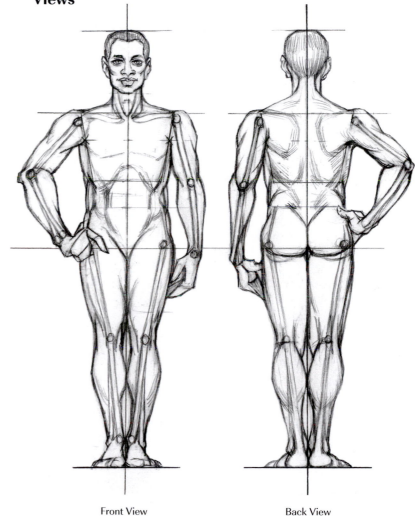

Front View   Back View

1-5 **Contouring Lines for the Female Body, Front and Back Views**

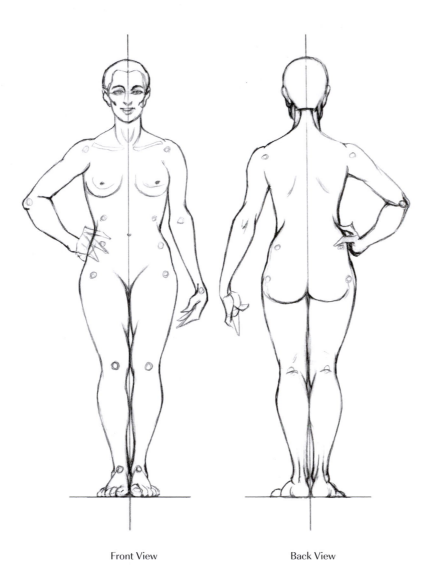

Front View   Back View

THE BASIC BONE STRUCTURE OF THE BODY

The bone structure in this book is symbolic and abstract. It is not my intention to copy the real human skeleton. My objective in using a simple and abstract bone structure is to make it easier to draw and understand, and easier to obtain the proper proportions of the figures. The shape of the human body is complex. To draw it well, you need to spend extensive time studying bones and muscles. Unfortunately, in most cases, theatre students don't have a long time to study the human anatomy. The simplified abstract bone structure used here is going to help students to better understand the human body and its movements (see Figure 1-6).

The skeleton dominates and directs all surfaces of the body, and the bone joints determine and dominate all the movements of the body. We must discuss the basic bone structure of the human body to understand body movements. To keep it clear and simple, my discussion is focused on the basic length and width of the outer edges of the skeleton, and on the major joints of the skeleton. The outer edges of the skeleton include the outline of the skull and the outline, or frame, of the chest and pelvis masses. The major joints include the spine, shoulder, elbow, wrist, hip/leg, knee, and ankle. In real life, the chest and pelvis are irregular shapes. In this book, I am going to use either boxes or abstract shapes to demonstrate the body parts. Small circles will be used for each joint. Abstract sticks will be used for the length of the bone. The length of the bones between the forearm and upper arm, and between the lower leg and thigh, may differ in real skeletons, but I will make them equal distances here because it will be easier to calculate the proportion ratio.

The Joints of the Body

Joints connect or hinge together two things. There are many joints on the human body. The spine joins the head mass, chest mass, and pelvis mass. The collarbone, shoulder blade, and arm are joined together at the shoulder and connected with the chest as a unit. Joints are capable of moving in many directions within their limitations. Each arm has its own joints: shoulder, elbow, wrist, and finger. Each leg also has its joints: hip, knee, ankle, and toe. Each joint directs body movements. In figure drawing, when joints are in the correct positions, they will show comfortable movements and body rhythm with natural expressiveness as a whole. Incorrect positions will make the figures seem stiff or lopsided. Through our experiences during our daily activities, we know how joints work. But showing the joints properly through drawing is critical and requires practice. The bone joints allow us to move our body parts comfortably and also inform us of the limitations of our joints. Consider and study how your own joints work; practice stick figure drawings to analyze the joint functions and limitations in different positions.

1-6 The Abstract Skeleton of the Body and Its Joints

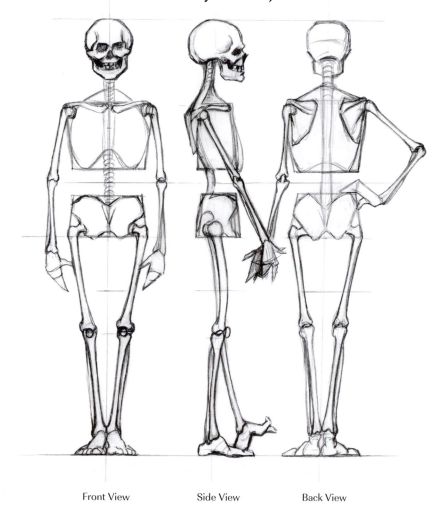

Front View   Side View   Back View

The Head, Chest, and Pelvis

There are three major masses of the human body — the head, chest, and pelvis. They are joined together by the spine, which controls the movements and turning directions of the head, chest, and pelvis. The significant fact here is that these three masses are able to move independently of one another (see Figure 1-7).

Making the three masses move in different directions will add dramatic excitement and personality to the figure. When the body moves, the balance has to be maintained. The proper angles between the body masses maintain this balance. The neck area of the spine usually has more flexibility than the lumbar spine. The flexible spine allows the head, chest, and pelvis to face up, down, or sideways, or to turn around. When each mass faces in different directions, you will see twisting movements.

When the body is in action, the body centerline becomes curved. This line can also be called the action line. When the body bends or twists, it creates angles or curves between each mass. If the body is in standing position, you will see the level of each mass forming a 90-degree right angle to the spine — the centerline of the body. When the body bends forward, it brings the front of the chest and the front of the pelvis close together to form an angle, while stretching the distance between the back of the chest and pelvis, forming a curved line. When the body bends to either side, it brings one side of the chest and one side of the pelvis close together, forming an angle between them, and stretches the dis-tance between the other side of the chest and pelvis, forming a curved line. You will see the same pattern when the body bends backward. When the body is in a twisting position, the body centerline and the outline of the body become curvy lines rather than sharp angles. The three masses can be turned and twisted in different directions within spine limita-tions, but the chest and pelvis always move in oppo-site directions from each other in order to keep the body in balance; otherwise, the body would fall.

A small turn of the body gives some action to the figure. A full or exaggerated turn or twisting of the

1-7 The Body Masses and Their Movements

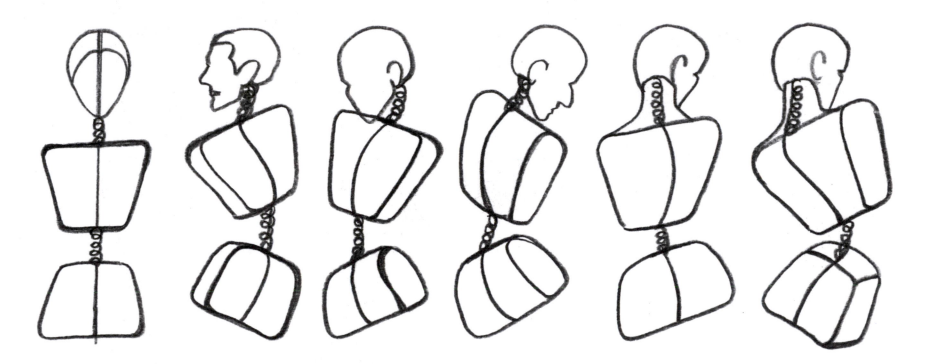

The head, chest, and pelvis are joined together by the spine and move independently of one another.
Make the blocks move in different directions to add dramatic excitement and personality to the figure.

body increases the dramatic action and attitude of the character, and gives a loud or screaming emotional statement. Try to manipulate these three masses by turning them in different directions, allowing them to speak for your characters' actions. When you make the three masses face different directions (see Figure 1-8), you will immediately see your character alive and active. It is essential in character drawing to establish the relationships of the head to the torso, the head to the neck, the head to the chest, and the chest to the pelvis. These relationships portray a great deal of the personality of the character.

1-8 Turning the Three Body Masses

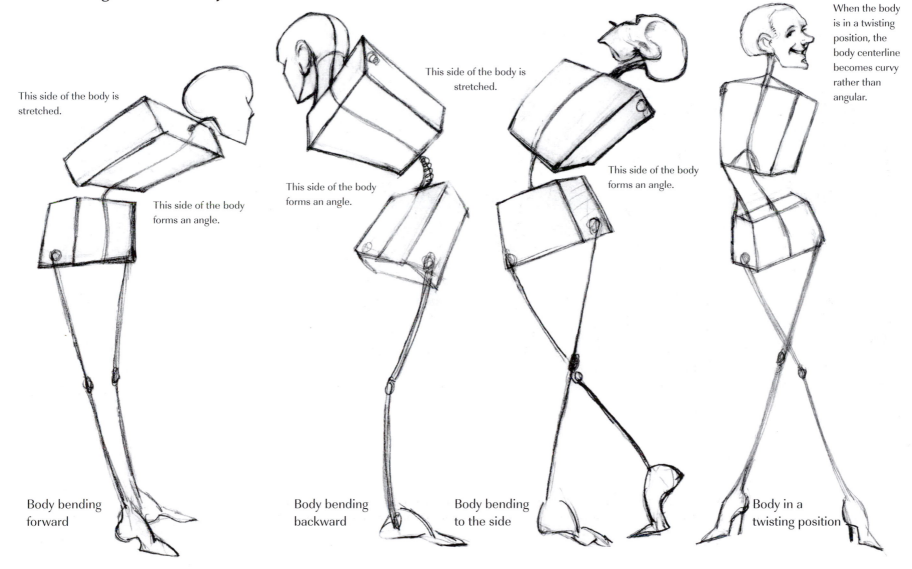

This side of the body is stretched.

This side of the body forms an angle.

This side of the body forms an angle.

This side of the body is stretched.

This side of the body forms an angle.

When the body is in a twisting position, the body centerline becomes curvy rather than angular.

Body bending forward

Body bending backward

Body bending to the side

Body in a twisting position

The Relationships between the Limbs and Body Masses

We have discussed how the arms are joined to the chest, and how the legs are joined to the hipbone/pelvis. Therefore, when the chest and pelvis move in different directions, the arms should follow the chest as a unit, and the legs should follow the pelvis as a unit. The limbs cannot be considered as separate objects from their units (see Figure 1-9). For example, when the body is in an erect standing position, the chest and pelvis masses are in horizontal lines parallel to each other. The joints of the shoulder, elbow, and wrist as well as the joints of the hip, knee, and ankle will be parallel to their units. But when the chest moves in a direction that makes the right side of the shoulder higher than the left side, the right shoulder and arm will go higher as well. When many students draw this position, they draw the arms at the same level. They forget the arms are connected to the chest mass.

Arm and leg movements also partially control the levels of the chest and pelvis. When one arm rises higher than the other arm, the shoulder of the rising arm will go higher. When one leg supports the weight of the body, this leg will push this side of the pelvis higher and in a tilted position. The pelvis can be pushed up because the flexible lumbar spine allows the pelvis to be tilted. The relaxed-leg side of the pelvis line and hipline will be dropped. The nonsupporting leg usually steps forward, keeping a relaxed or bending position to compensate for the length of the weighted leg and the drop of the pelvis mass.

Most costume designers create their figures for designing costumes without live models. They draw the figures from their heads or from reference books or magazines. Once you understand how the human structure and joints work, you will feel at ease and comfortable with your drawings. You will be able to create your own characters of motion in a variety of positions in order to demonstrate the costumes and personalities of the roles in the play.

THE BALANCE OF THE BODY

The human body is uniquely and symmetrically balanced. The human body also has a natural balance ability. The weight of the body often swings back and forth from one leg to the other when the body is walking. When the body is turning or twisting, it creates angles and curves in order to keep the body balanced. This principle is like the balance in a sculptured object. If the bottom portion of the sculpture leans to one side, then the top portion of the sculpture must lean in the opposite direction to maintain the balance of the whole piece. To create a more sophisticated sense of movements or actions, define the body language by employing twisted angles and curves faced in different directions. To keep the body well-balanced, locate the center of gravity for the figure. These are the important elements in helping us understand and draw human figures. Keep the movement liquid and the balance solid.

Weight on Both Legs

The spine is the centerline of the body, from where all body parts are symmetrically balanced. The joints of the body are lined up and parallel to each other. Due to the force of gravity, no matter how the body moves, there is always a center of gravity line from the pit of the neck directly down to the ground. This gravity line will never change to curved or angled, but the body centerline will change to curved when the body is in action.

1-9 The Relationships between the Limbs and the Three Masses

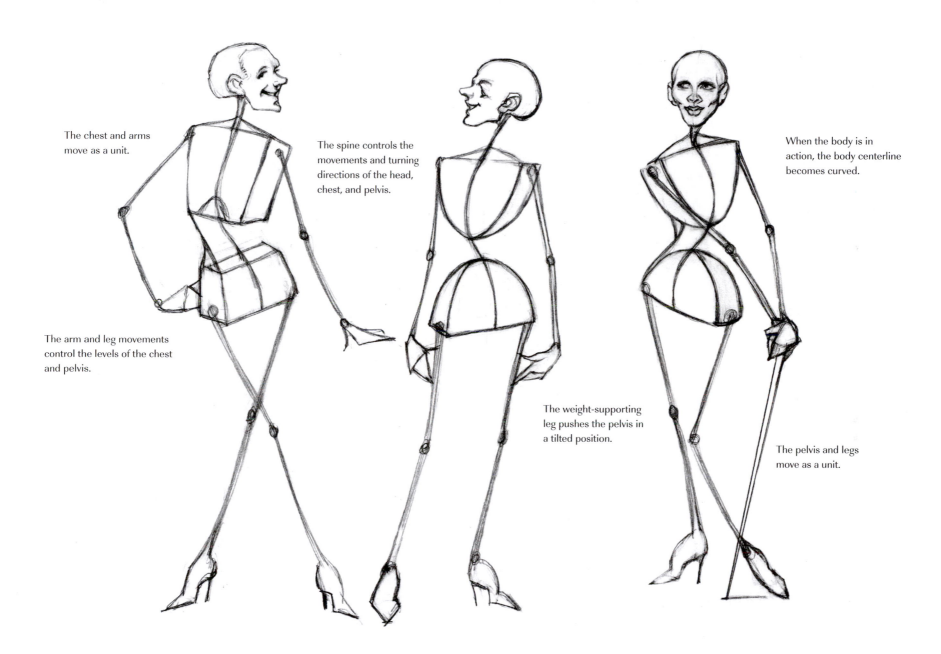

The chest and arms move as a unit.

The spine controls the movements and turning directions of the head, chest, and pelvis.

When the body is in action, the body centerline becomes curved.

The arm and leg movements control the levels of the chest and pelvis.

The weight-supporting leg pushes the pelvis in a tilted position.

The pelvis and legs move as a unit.

When the body is standing straight, all body weight is distributed equally on two legs (see Figure 1-10). The body centerline is straight. The center of gravity line overlaps with the body center-line, starting from the pit of the neck and extending directly down between the middle of the two feet to the ground, whether the feet are in a closed or open position. All the horizontal lines (the shoulder line, bustline, waistline, pelvis line, hipline) are parallel to the ground and form 90-degree angles with the body centerline.

Figures 1-11 through 1-16 are design samples showing weight on both legs.

1-10   Weight on Both Legs

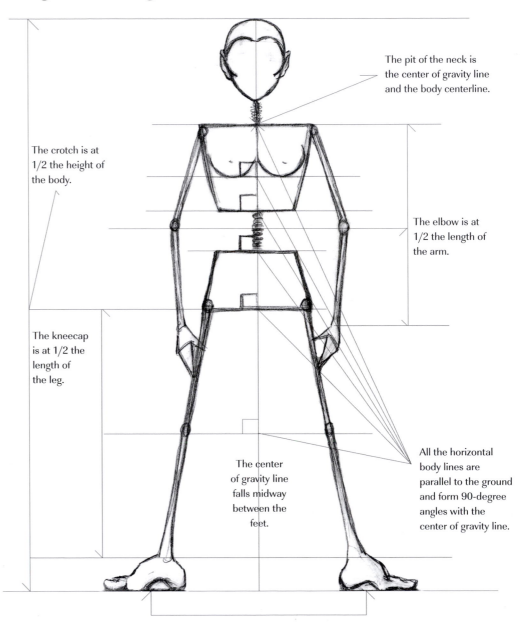

The pit of the neck is the center of gravity line and the body centerline.

The crotch is at 1/2 the height of the body.

The elbow is at 1/2 the length of the arm.

The kneecap is at 1/2 the length of the leg.

The center of gravity line falls midway between the feet.

All the horizontal body lines are parallel to the ground and form 90-degree angles with the center of gravity line.

The weight on both legs

1-11 **Design Sample of Weight on Both Legs —** *Look Homeward, Angel*

1-12 **Design Sample of Weight on Both Legs —** *Look Homeward, Angel*

Luke
Act II

LOOK HOMEWARD, ANGEL
UCF DEPARTMENT OF THEATRE
SPRING 2002

Dr. Maguire
Act I & II

Dr. Maguire
Act II

LOOK HOMEWARD, ANGEL
UCF DEPARTMENT OF THEATR
SPRING 2002

1-13   **Design Sample of Weight on Both Legs — *Tintypes***

1-14   **Design Sample of Weight on Both Legs — *Tintypes***

1-15 Design Sample of Weight on Both Legs — *Tintypes*

1-16 Design Sample of Weight on Both Legs — *Tintypes*

Weight on One Leg

Weight on one leg is a common pose for costume design figure drawings (see Figure 1-17). It gives the figure characteristic action and attitude for showing the costumes. There are many designs using one leg support, but the principle of balancing the body is the same. When the body weight shifts to one leg, the pelvis swings out to the side of the weight-supporting leg. The swing causes the body centerline to become curved and separate from the center of gravity line (the center of gravity line overlaps with the body centerline in the two-leg support pose). This curved body centerline is considered an action line as well. The degree of the curve is based on half or full actions/movements. A half action/movement will show a soft or shallow curve at the body centerline; a full action/movement will show a deeper curve at the body centerline. To balance the body so it doesn't fall, the weight-supporting foot will naturally be located where the center of gravity line ends on the ground. We discussed that the center of gravity line goes directly down from the pit of the neck to the ground. Therefore, the weight-supporting foot should be located there. This is a rule for balancing the body in figure drawings. You will read similar information in all art books on figure drawings. The center of gravity line is the key to balancing the body, figuring out a stable-standing figure, and checking if the weight-supporting foot is in the correct location — where the center of gravity line ends on the ground.

1-17 Weight on One Leg

The pit of the neck is at the center of the gravity line and the body centerline.

The body centerline

The shoulder line, the bustline, and the bottom of the rib cage are parallel.

The rib cage and the pelvis are tilted in opposite directions.

The body's swinging motion causes the body centerline to become curved and separated from the center of gravity line.

The weight-supporting leg pushes up the pelvis to a tilted position.

The pelvis line, the hipline, and the kneecap line are parallel.

The weight-supporting foot is located where the center of gravity line ends on the ground.

The weight on one leg

We discussed how the chest and pelvis masses work and the relationship between the limbs and the masses. I will highlight the important points one more time: The head, chest, and pelvis are joined by the spine but move independently to offer us a variety of bodily movements and positions. When body weight is on one leg, this side of the pelvis swings out and tilts toward the relaxed leg because the weight-supporting leg pushes the pelvis up. The relaxed side of the pelvis drops down, and the joined leg follows. The knee and ankle of this leg will be lower than the knee and ankle of the weight-supporting leg. The nonsupporting leg may also be in a bending or relaxed position.

When the pelvis tilts to one side, the chest will tilt in the opposite direction in order to balance the body. This creates an angle between the chest and pelvis and causes the body centerline to be curved. The shoulder line, armpit line, bustline, elbows, wrists, and hands are parallel. In the pelvis unit, the pelvis line, hipline, kneecaps, and ankles are parallel and move in the same directions because the pelvis and legs are a unit, just like the chest and arms are a unit. When they move, they move together as a whole.

Figures 1-18 through 1-24 are design samples showing weight on one leg.

1-18 **Design Sample of Weight on One Leg—*Tintypes***

1-19 Design Sample of Weight on One Leg—*Tintypes*

1-20 Design Sample of Weight on One Leg—*Tintypes*

1-21   **Design Sample of Weight on One Leg—*Tintypes***

1-22   **Design Sample of Weight on One Leg—*Tintypes***

1-23 Design Sample of Weight on One Leg—*Tintypes*

1-24 Design Sample of Weight on One Leg — *Laundry and Bourbon*

Body Leaning on an Object

When the body leans on something (see Figure 1-25), the body centerline also changes from straight to curved because part of the body weight is distributed to lean on the object. In this case, the center of the gravity line will fall down somewhere between the object and the body. Where? It really depends on the distance between the leaning body and the object. In general, if the feet of the leaning body are close to the object, the center of gravity line should be near the feet; if the feet of the leaning body are farther away from the object, then the center of gravity line will be located between the feet and object.

In conclusion, when you draw a figure leaning on an object, you should emphasize the action lines, the angles between the body and the object, and the relationships between the three masses and limbs. For a body leaning on an object, drawing the foot or feet at the center of gravity line will not work.

Figures 1-26 through 1-29 show design samples of bodies leaning on an object.

1-25 Body Leaning on an Object

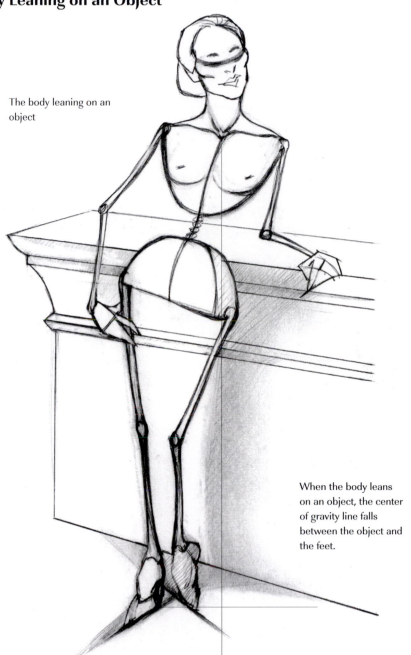

The body leaning on an object

When the body leans on an object, the center of gravity line falls between the object and the feet.

1-26 Design Sample of Body Leaning on an Object—
Lone Star

1-27 Design Sample of Body Leaning on an Object—
Lone Star

1-28 **Design Sample of Body Leaning on an Object**—*Laundry and Bourbon*

1-29 **Design Sample of Body Leaning on an Object**—*Laundry and Bourbon*

FIGURES IN ACTION

We all know that when we design costumes we should have a concept. For me, the concept involves not only designing garments but also, equally important, creating the figure poses. I apply symmetrical balance to draw body features, but I use asymmetrical balance to design the figure poses. I want my characters to tell stories and possess personalities. However, I never forget that costume design is always the main subject to express. My theory is that characteristic bodies with interesting and perhaps exaggerated features can make the costumes even more interesting, eye-catching, elegant, practical, and meaningful.

Abstract Stick Figures in Action

I often use abstract stick figures to establish the poses for my costume designs (see Figures 1-30 and 1-31). I work without live models, from my own imagination. I use tapered boxes or irregular shapes, sticks, and little circles to indicate the basic bone structure of the figures. That is the way I analyze and explore human body movements. This is always the fundamental thing to do: Get correct proportions, design action movements, locate the joints, and balance the weight of the body. This approach helps me to modify the body movements, actions, or attitudes that define the body as being alive. The greatest benefit of using abstract shapes in poses is that doing so will eliminate a lot of meandering lines and shapes that don't say anything about the charac-

ter. The most important element in drawing a figure is to establish the body frame before proceeding with the details. The tendency to start a figure in detail at one spot and then proceed to the end usually causes incorrect proportions and uncontrolled figure placement on the page.

When the body is in action, the centerline of the body will be curved, as we discussed before. Properly showing the degrees of the angles and what directions the curves point toward are the foundations for creating body movements and actions. Clearly define the locations of the joints, such as the shoulders, elbows, wrists, hip bones, knees, ankles, and feet, in action. To create dynamic action figures, it is necessary to analyze the body action line, the joints and parts, and to manipulate them by twisting, turning, and bending in order to make them move with

1-30 Abstract Stick Figures in Action

exciting and dynamic actions. The twisting of the body and the use of the weight-bearing foot give a definite spirit to figures that entertain. To emphasize strong angles between the head, chest, and pelvis, use straight lines against curved lines, and round shapes against angular shapes. This will put motion and energy into your figure while capturing the spirit and soul of the character.

Contouring the Stick Figure

Studying the terms and functions of muscles may require a full semester or more. My approach for contouring the figure is to just focus on the silhouette of the muscles and simplify them as straight or curved lines, and angular or round shapes. Apply these lines and shapes to the figure as a format pattern. Study and analyze the outlines of the body to perceive the following: which body part outlines are relatively straight or curved, which show angular shapes, which generally stay forward, and which generally stay behind. The outlines of the human body overlap one another in different shapes, angles, and lines, to form the human framework.

The muscle tissue around the joints of the body is thin, allowing the joints to move. They can be seen as angular shapes, or knobs, and indentations. In figure drawing, we must indicate and locate these visible joints and bones to avoid the look of a rubber dummy. The human body is symmetrically and mechanically built. All body actions and movements are directed and controlled by mechanical joints. Inadequately defining the joints, consequently, will not show natural proper movements, and lack a sense of reality and authenticity.

In general, joints appear more noticeable in a thinner or bonier body. If the joints are covered by thick fat tissue, as in a heavier body, this will limit the body movements and the body will show more rounded, curved lines and shapes. When contouring a thin or bony figure, you should emphasize the angular bone structure with firmer, smaller muscles. When drawing a heavy figure, emphasize the roundness and ample flesh more than the bone structures.

1-31 Abstract Stick Figures in Action

CONTOURING THE STICK FIGURE FROM HEAD TO FEET

Contouring the Head Contour the head as egg-shaped and the neck as cylinder-shaped (see Figure 1-32). Note the male's jawline has a more angular shape than the female's. The neck portion is at the top part of the spine. The front and back views of the spine are straight lines; from the profile, the spine creates an S-curved silhouette. The spine curves toward the front, and the head sits on the top end of the spine.

While contouring the neck, follow the direction of the spine and treat the neck as a slanted-forward cylinder. From the profile, notice that the top of the front part of the neck starts just below the chin and ends at the pit of the neck. The top of the back part of the neck starts at the same level as the bottom of the ear and merges with the shoulder slope. Thus, the base of the front of the neck starts lower and ends lower than the back of the neck. From the profile view, the female neck should resemble a diamond shape and the male neck should resemble an elongated diamond shape or parallelogram, due to males having thicker necks. In the front and back views, the outlines of the neck are straight. A pair of prominent muscles, called the sternocleidomastoid muscles, are set symmetrically at each side of the neck. They start from just behind the ear and slant down to the middle of the collarbone. The functions of these muscles are to support the head and turn it in different directions. The female neck is thinner with smoother visible neck muscles, whereas the male neck is thicker and more muscular. The collarbone lays flat at the shoulder line, and its two ends meet at the center of the base of the neck. This intersection forms a deep indentation called the pit of the neck, which is used as a pivotal point for figure poses.

1-32 Contouring the Head and Neck

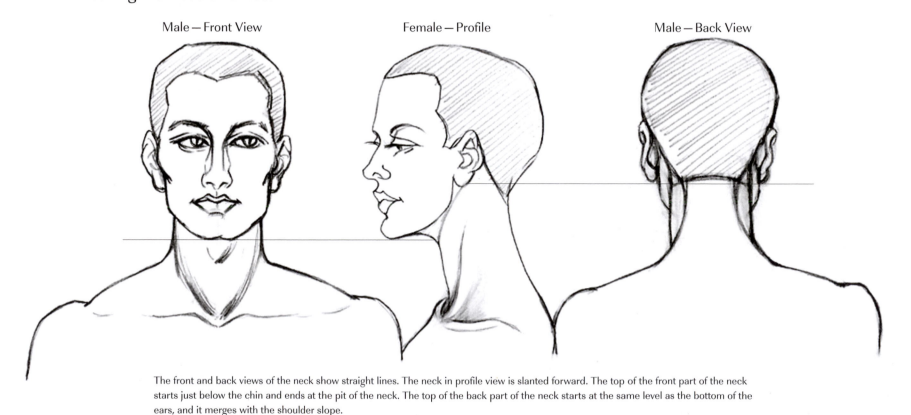

Male — Front View   Female — Profile   Male — Back View

The front and back views of the neck show straight lines. The neck in profile view is slanted forward. The top of the front part of the neck starts just below the chin and ends at the pit of the neck. The top of the back part of the neck starts at the same level as the bottom of the ears, and it merges with the shoulder slope.

There are three common mistakes when drawing the neck: drawing the profile of the neck as a straight cylinder, rather than a slanted cylinder; drawing the neck as a tapered cylinder (funnel-shaped), instead of using parallel lines; and using sharp angles as the neck merges into the shoulder, instead of soft curves. The neck is a small part of the whole body, but it plays a very significant role for creating character drawings because it expresses emotions and movements. Therefore, we have to pay considerable attention to contouring the neck. The indentations on the neck should be emphasized in order to depict a graceful, elegant, and healthy neck. The outlines of the side of the neck are straight (in front and back views) and can be drawn in one complete line with the shoulder slope, or with a break where the neck and shoulder slope meet. In this case, the shoulder-slope lines should stay behind the necklines. The slope is slightly curved toward the shoulder bone.

Contouring the Torso Referring to Figure 1-33, use round curved lines to draw female breasts and soft curved lines for the waist. Use angular and sculpted lines to draw the muscular male chest, and slightly curved lines for the waistline. Define the edge of the pelvis and hipbone. The contouring line for the center-front crotch forms a curved V-shaped line and starts above the crotch line. Rear cheek lines are an upside-down curved V-shaped line and are located a little bit below the crotch line.

Contouring the Arms Divide the arm into three sections — the shoulder, biceps, and forearm. When drawing female arms, use one continuous line to emphasize the smoothness. When drawing male arms, use broken lines to emphasize more sculpted muscles. If broken lines are used for the arm, the shoulder and forearm lines should stay in front of (overlap) the biceps lines. The elbow contains wrin-

1-33 Contouring the Torso

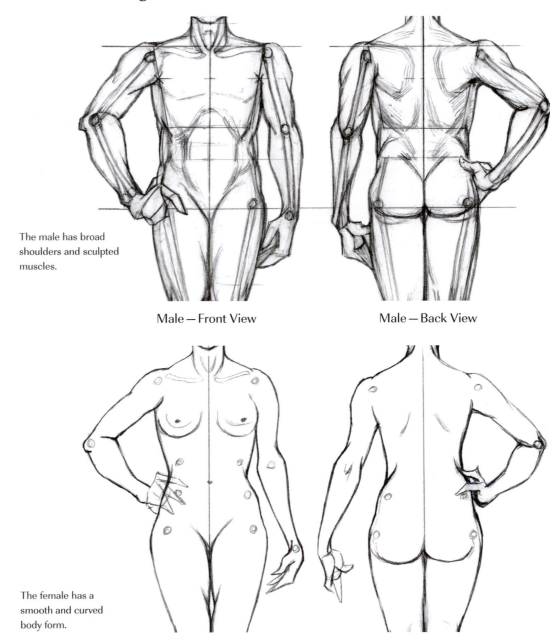

The male has broad shoulders and sculpted muscles.

Male — Front View

Male — Back View

The female has a smooth and curved body form.

Female — Front View

Female — Back View

kled flesh and shows the elbow joint. The front of the elbow forms a natural bending line at the middle of the arm. The forearm tapers down to the wrist; the outer curve (side) of the forearm starts above the elbow bending line with a somewhat greater curve. The inner side of the forearm starts just below the elbow bending line. (See Figure 1-34.)

Contouring the Legs and Feet When contouring the legs and feet, refer to Figure 1-35. The curved V-shaped line at the front of the crotch is where the leg muscles start. Use curved lines to draw the thigh and the lower leg, and use straight lines for the knee area. The thigh portion is thicker and fuller than the lower leg; the knee area contains less muscle. The lower leg tapers down to the ankle; the calves are full and firm, and the bottom of the calf line ends at the halfway point of the lower leg.

Keep three main curves in focus: the thigh, calf, and ankle. In the front view, the inner outline of the leg is straighter (with soft curves) than the outer outline of the leg. There is an indentation curve at the middle of the inner thigh because that is where the sartorius muscle overlaps the gracilis muscle. The inner thigh line can be drawn with three broken lines: upper thigh, lower thigh, and lower leg. The upper thigh line stops at mid-thigh. Then the lower thigh line starts on top of it and continues and ends just below the knee.

The lower leg line starts behind the lower thigh line and curves down to the ankle. The outer outline of the leg can be done with three broken lines: thigh, knee, and lower leg. The thigh has a big curve, starts from the hips, and stops at the knee level. The outer outline of the knee joint is relatively straight and stays behind both the thigh and lower leg lines; an indentation mark can be used to indicate the kneecap position. Be sure to attentively mold the calf curves and anklebones. The

1-34 Contouring the Arms

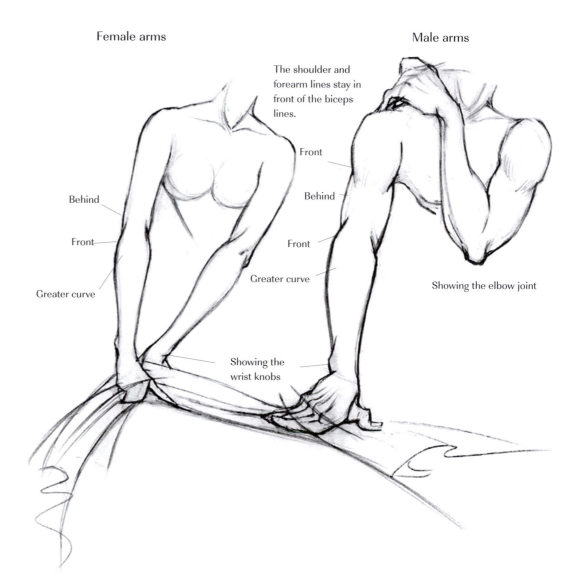

Female arms

Male arms

The shoulder and forearm lines stay in front of the biceps lines.

Front

Behind

Front

Greater curve

Behind

Front

Greater curve

Showing the elbow joint

Behind

Greater curve

Showing the wrist knobs

The outer curve of the forearm starts above the elbow. The inner curve of the forearm starts just below the elbow bending line. The outer line of the forearm is more curved than the inner line. Female arms are smoother than male arms.

fullest curve point of the outer calf is higher than the fullest curve point of the inner calf. The inner anklebone curve is higher than the outer anklebone curve. If you draw a line at the fullest point of the calf from the inner calf line to the outer calf line and draw another line from the inner ankle to the outer ankle, you will see that the two lines are headed toward opposite directions. (see Figure 1-35).

In profile view, the leg is not a straight vertical line. The front of the thigh curved line is the most forward of the leg outlines. The next most prominent curve is the calf. The outlines of the back thigh and shin are straighter with soft curves. The back view of the leg will have the same silhouette as the front view, except the back view will have a bending line in the back of the knee and tendon lines going down to the heel. The back of the heel is a ball-like curve and merges with the tendon lines that continue up to the leg. Contour the arch bone with arch lines, and use small curves for the toes.

Finally the female leg has smaller, softer calves. Male legs have more muscular calves. Bring to life realistic human legs by shaping and accentuating joints and natural curves.

Figures 1-36 through 1-43 contain design samples of contoured bodies.

1-35 Contouring the Legs and Feet

Leg front view   Leg profile   Leg back view

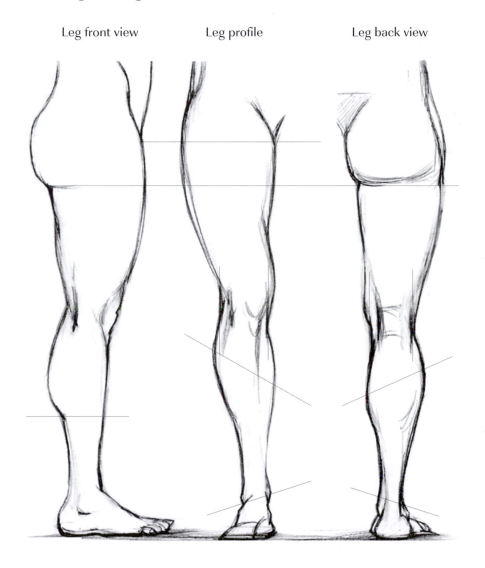

The rear cheek line is lower than the center-front crotch. The thigh and calf areas have more flesh and show curvy lines. The knee area has less flesh and forms straight lines. The calf line ends at the halfway point of the leg. The fullest curve point of the outer calf is higher than the fullest curve point of the inner calf. The inner anklebone is higher; the outer anklebone is lower.

1-36 **Design Sample of Contoured Bodies** — *Crazy for You*

1-37 **Design Sample of Contoured Bodies—*Crazy for You***

1-38   **Design Sample of Contoured Bodies — *Crazy for You***

1-39 Design Sample of Contoured Bodies—*The Dance & The Railroad*

1-40 Design Sample of Contoured Bodies—*The Dance & The Railroad*

CORNELL UNIVERSITY
DEPARTMENT OF THEATRE ARTS
THE DANCE & THE RAILROAD
Ma

CORNELL UNIVERSITY
DEPARTMENT OF THEATRE ARTS
THE DANCE & THE RAILROAD
Lone

1-41   **Design Sample of Contoured Bodies**—*The Butterfingers Angel*

THE BUTTERFINGERS ANGEL
UCF THEATRE
Fall 1998

COW   DONKEY   SHEEP

1-42 **Design Sample of Contoured Bodies—** *The Butterfingers Angel*

1-43 Design Sample of Contoured Bodies—*Dracula*

DRACULA

Vampire Wives
DRACULA
COSTUME DESIGN BY TOM HUADXIANG
CENTRAL WASHINGTON UNIVERSITY

FIGURES IN DANCE

Keep the words *stretching, flowing,* and *rhythm* in mind to accentuate the image of dancing. Dancers' bodies possess rhythm, balance, strength, distinction, and flexibility. Their powerful shoulders, backs, and elegant limbs are firmly muscled.

Correctly locating the weight-supporting leg in relation to the body is the key to balancing the body. Dance poses can be one-leg support or two-leg support, but keep in mind that the center of gravity line is the guideline for positioning the weight-supporting leg or legs. This principle is also utilized in the action figures we discussed earlier. Again, where a line from the pit of the neck falls directly down to the ground is the center of gravity line, which is the location for the weight-supporting leg/legs. As I mentioned before, this principle cannot be applied to a body leaning on an object. This center of gravity line applies to dance figures as well. The differences are the following: when the dance body bends forward, the center of gravity line shifts in front of the weight-supporting leg; when the dance body bends to the side, the center of gravity line descends to the side of the weight-supporting leg; when the body bends to the back, the center of gravity line moves to the back of the weight-supporting leg. The deeper the bending angle, the farther the distance between the gravity line and the weight-supporting leg.

Use the head, torso, and supporting leg to maintain a firm and active posture. Use the stretching limbs to sustain the body's rhythm and balance. A dancer's body is stronger and more flexible than that of the average person. Keep in mind that the head, chest, and pelvis are three masses that move independently; this allows you to create exaggerated and stretched-out poses by manipulating the three masses. The feet and legs are naturally joined together at nearly a 90-degree angle to support the body weight.

In dance, the relaxed leg is commonly stretched either forward or backward and reaches to its full extent. When the leg is in a stretching position, the angle between the foot and leg dramatically changes. This stretching position diminishes the angle degree between the foot and the leg as the lines become straighter. The toes are pointed and curved downward, which causes the heel to be pulled backward. The foot in this pointed position can be seen in many dance poses. The hand positions are opposite from the feet. The angles between the wrists and hands expand. The feet are drawn tense and tight, but the hands are usually more relaxed, graceful, and sophisticated.

Dancing bodies possess sculptured expressions of dynamics. To express sculptured and powerful characteristics, stress the movements of the head and torso and create an impression of powerful limbs. A real dancer controls his or her body's balance, but when you draw, *you* control the dancer's balance.

Figures 1-44 through 1-52 show abstract figures in dance. Figures 1-53 through 1-60 provide design sketches of figures in dance.

1-44 Abstract Stick Figures in Dance

1-45 Abstract Stick Figures in Dance

1-46 **Abstract Stick Figures in Dance**

1-47   Abstract Stick Figures in Dance

1-48 Figure in Dance

1-49 Figure in Dance

1-50 **Figure in Dance**

1-51 **Figure in Dance**

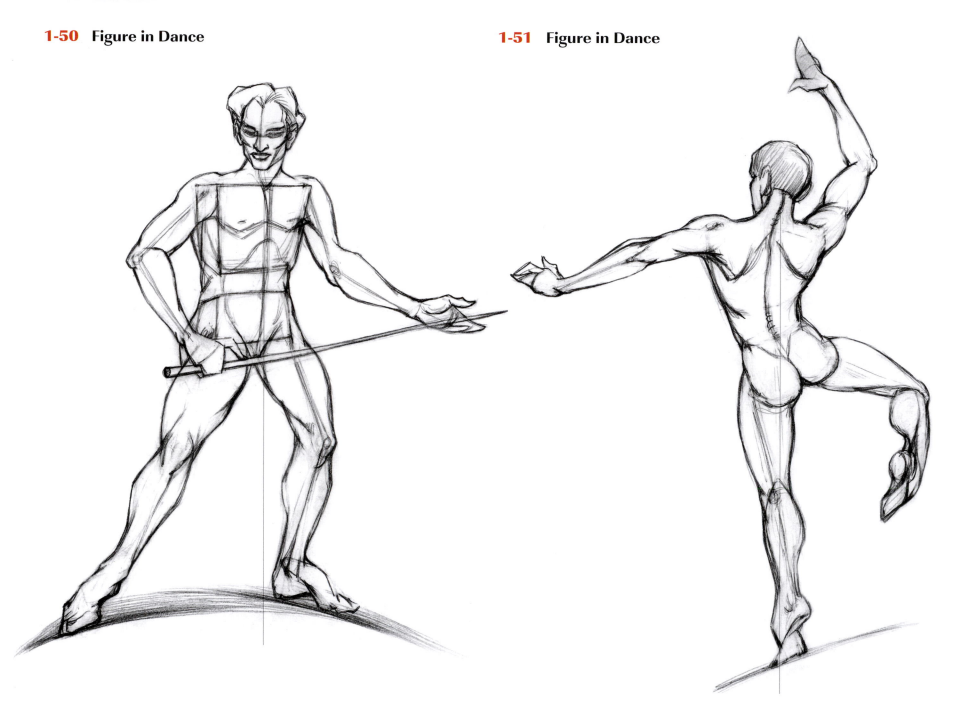

1-52 **Figure in Dance**

1-53   **Design Sample of Figures in Dance** — *Crazy for You*

1-54 **Design Sample of Figures in Dance—*Crazy for You***

1-55   **Design Sample of Figures in Dance—*Crazy for You***

1-56 **Design Sample of Figures in Dance—*Crazy for You***

1-57   **Design Sample of Figures in Dance—***Dance '91*

1-58   **Design Sample of Figures in Dance—***Dance '91*

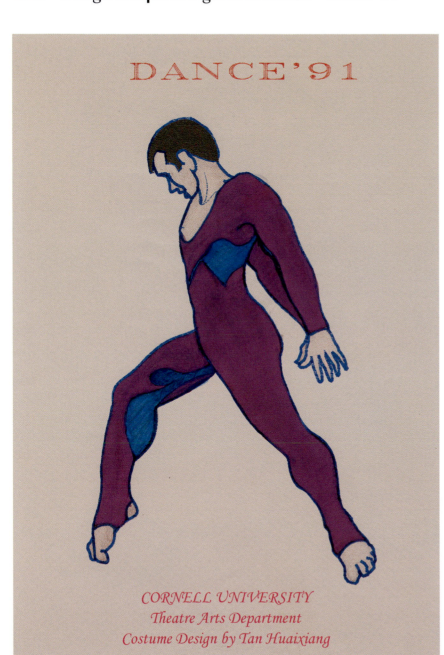

1-59   **Design Sample of Figures in Dance—*Dance '91***

DANCE'91

Costume Design by Tan Huaixiang
at CORNELL UNIVERSITY

1-60 **Design Sample of Figures in Dance—***Dance '91*

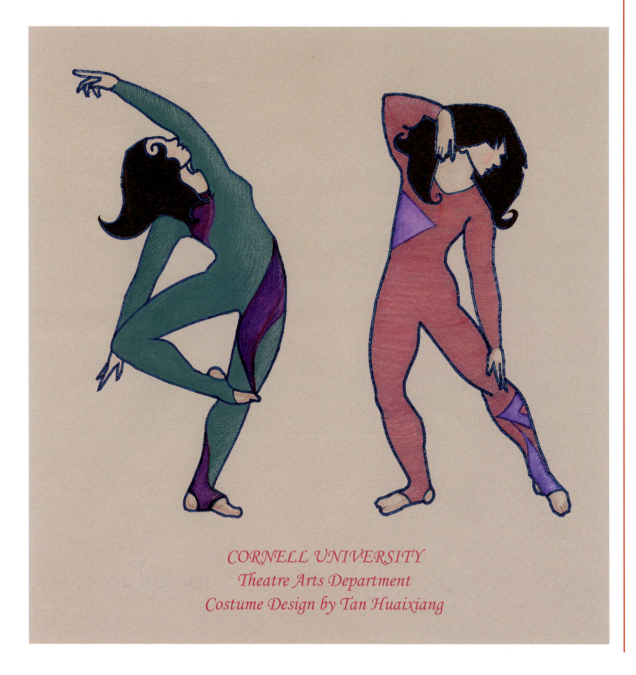

CORNELL UNIVERSITY
Theatre Arts Department
Costume Design by Tan Huaixiang

FIGURE POSES CHANGE THROUGH TIME AND FASHION

Keep two important ideas in mind when creating figure poses: one, use the poses or gestures that will express the character's personality; and two, use the poses or gestures that will show your costume designs at their finest. As costume designers, we must combine costume history and fashion styles in order to develop many different poses. Fashion has changed often and dramatically over thousands of years and involves tastes, opinions, culture, religion, geography, location, and technology. The development of economic societies and technological inventions has influenced clothing styles. The clothing is made for the body, and the body is a frame for supporting the clothing or garment. In my opinion, these two elements cannot be separated. A certain style requires specific poses to carry out and represent the garment's best appearance.

Each time period in fashion holds its own appreciation of the beautiful. Women wore corsets throughout the centuries to flatten or accentuate the breasts, cinch waists, or pad shoulders; today, women get breast implants for a pair of full, large breasts. Trends affect men as well. In the past, men wore corsets, cinched their waists, and padded their shoulders, chests, and calves to achieve aesthetic standards; today, men go to gyms to exercise and gain muscle mass to meet today's standard of beauty — a muscular and healthy appearance.

Performance-major students take period movement and dialogue courses that are designed to allow their bodies and voices to adapt to roles in a period production. Costume designers should create suitable body frames for characters that will accent garments for that period and produce believable characters that will enhance the costume design.

Head-to-toe figures in three-quarter-view poses are usually the best for presenting expressive costumes because they show front, side, and partial-back views. Figures 1-61 through 1-69 are interpretations of my understanding of historical periods. They are based upon historical sources and references to frescoes, paintings, and sculptures. The figures displayed are from the Egyptian period to the present. Figures 1-70 through 1-76 are design samples that show how figure poses change through time and fashion.

1-61 Egyptian Figures

1-62 **Greek and Roman Figures**

1-63 **Medieval-Period Figures**

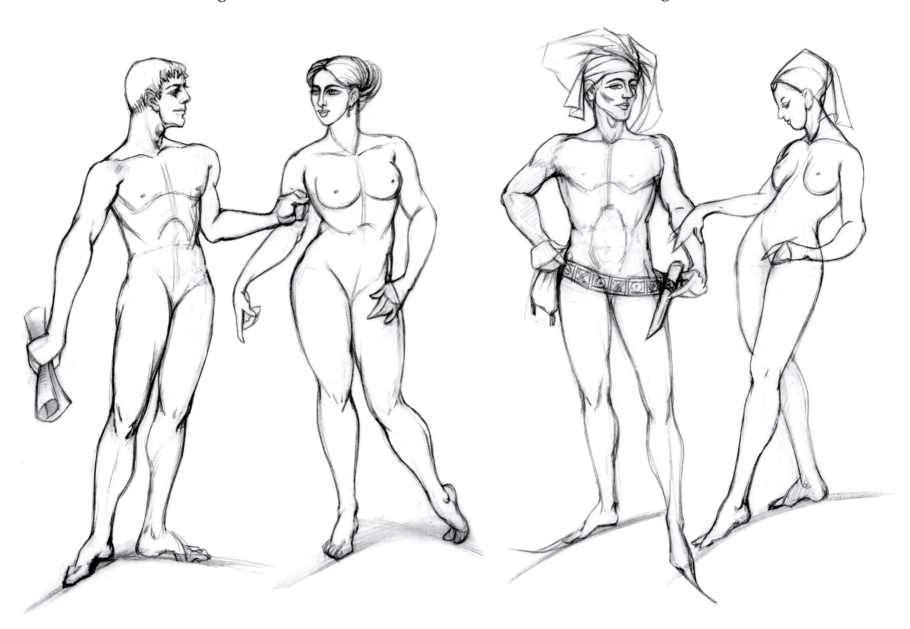

1-64 **Renaissance-Period Figures**

1-65 **Elizabethan-Period Figures**

1-66 18th-Century Figures

1-67 19th-Century Figures

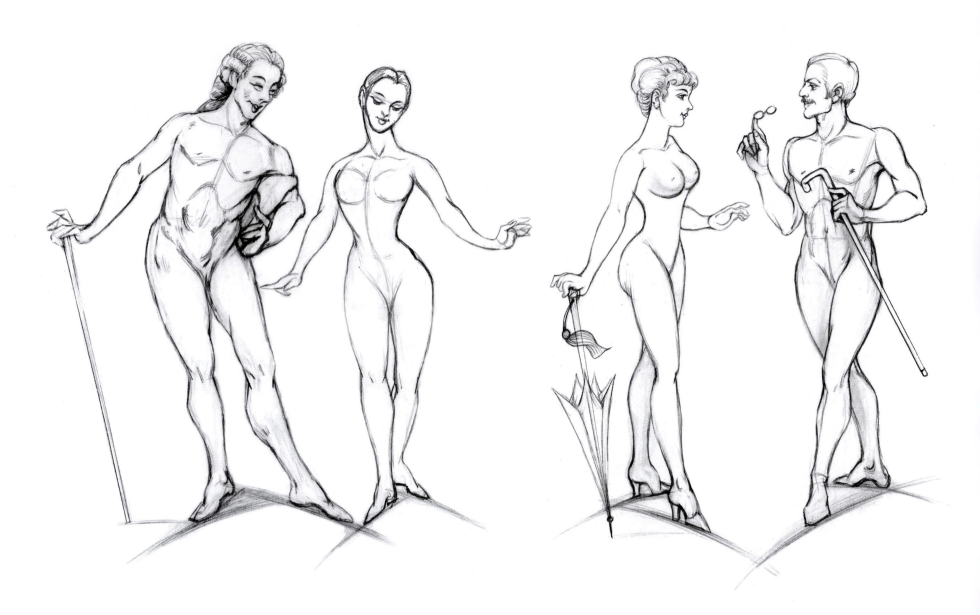

1-68 **20th-Century Figures**

1-69 **21st-Century Figures**

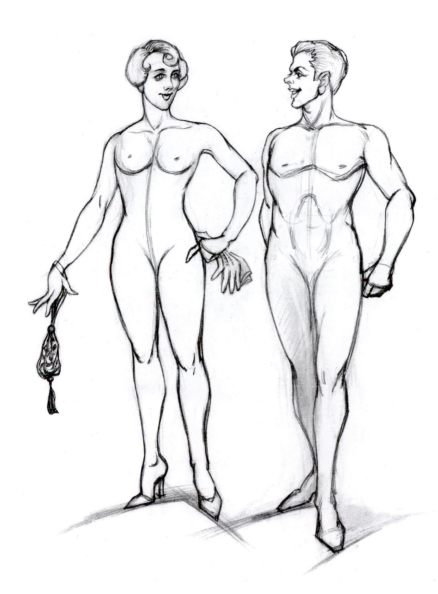

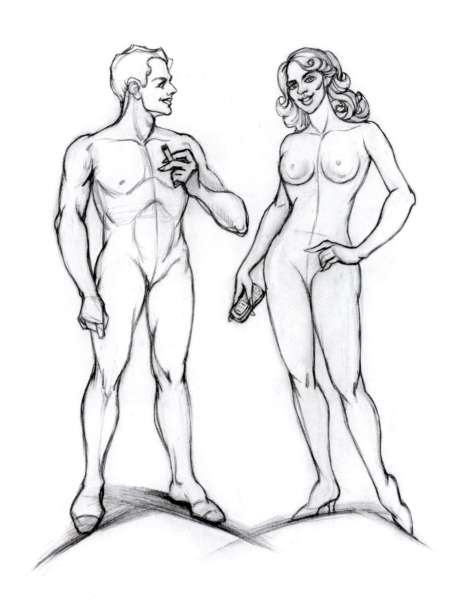

1-70 Design Sample—Figure Poses Change through Time and Fashion; Class Work

1-71 Design Sample—Figure Poses Change through Time and Fashion; Class Work

COSTUME DESIGN
CLASS WORK
By Tan Huaixiang

86. 5. 15
历史服装

COSTUME DESIGN
CLASS WORK
by Tan Huaixiang

1986. 5. 15.
历史服装

1-72 Design Sample—Figure Poses Change through Time and Fashion; *The Lion in Winter*

1-73 Design Sample—Figure Poses Change through Time and Fashion; *The Lion in Winter*

THE LION IN WINTER
ELEANOR

THE LION IN WINTER
ALAIS
ACT I SCENE 1~4
ACT II SCENE 3

1-74 Design Sample—Figure Poses Change through Time and Fashion; *Little Shop of Horrors*

1-75 Design Sample—Figure Poses Change through Time and Fashion; *The Merchant of Venice*

1-76 Design Sample—Figure Poses Change through Time and Fashion; *The Merchant of Venice*

The Prince of Morocco
THE MERCHANT OF VENICE

Portia
THE MERCHANT OF VENICE
TAN HUAIXIANG

GARMENTS AND TEXTURES IN RELATION TO THE BODY IN ACTION

The particular actions you decide for your figures should express the characters' personalities, and should communicate and enhance the meaning of the garments to their best advantage. Otherwise, the figure poses will lose their significant purpose. The purpose of defining body joints and contouring body silhouettes is to find what the figure is doing beneath the garment. The wrinkles and folds that appear on the garments are formed from beneath, where body joints are located.

Wrinkles and folds will bring a sense of reality to a body in action. When the body moves, the wrinkles and folds increase and become more visible, and they always follow the body action forms. It is not necessary to indicate all the detailed wrinkles and folds, since there are so many. You should just draw major ones to emphasize the actions. Wrinkles and folds are located where joints move (see Figure 1-77). We see them around armpits, elbow and knee bending areas, under busts, at waistlines, and around crotch areas. When body parts bend, they form folds at the inner bending area and produce pulling wrinkles as they radiate from the outer bending area. When the body is in less action, the garments show fewer folds and wrinkles. In this case, just draw a few strokes at the joint areas to define where the joints are, for a more realistic impression.

When drawing garments, be aware of several factors. Realize that collars, especially high ones, go around the neck even though the back of the collar is not visible; and collars must stay on top of the shoulder-slope lines. Never make straight horizontal lines across the three-dimensional body form because the human body consists of thick and thin

cylinder shapes. For example, when you draw the cuffs of sleeves and pants, skirt hems, or clothing across the chest, waist, and hipline, you should follow the body contour lines to outline the garments. When a garment touches or rests on the body, it reveals the body contours or silhouettes, so show some

1-77 Wrinkles and Folds Are Located Where Joints Move

stresses on the surface of the garment by developing visible wrinkles or folds (see Figure 1-78). When the garment falls away from the body, the body parts are hidden underneath the garment, but joints are revealed where the falling point starts. For example, when the arm stretches out to the side, the sleeve

rests on the outer arm contour line while the under arm contour line is hidden inside the sleeve. Some wrinkles will appear on the top of the sleeve, revealing the shape of the arm. If the arm bends, the surface of the sleeve will reveal the elbow knob because the elbow will touch the sleeve. The elbow is where the material will fall away from the body, so it is the fall-away starting point. The inner angle of the elbow will show several folds on the sleeve at the bending area; the angle of the outer bending area may show pulling wrinkles radiating from the elbow. The same principle applies to bending legs and swinging hips. If the garment is a short-sleeved shirt, the shoulder will be the fall-away point. The hip will be the fall-away point for short skirts and shorts.

Use different types of lines to express and accent the textures of garments. The wrinkles and folds can be sharp, crisp strokes; soft, fine, flowing strokes; or thick and bold strokes. Crisp strokes express angular folds to give the garment a full silhouette. Soft, fine, flowing strokes reveal more body curves because the material usually clings to the body (see Figure 1-79). The strokes also show the texture of the material. Thick, bold strokes show bulkiness and bluntness, and they give a full and massive silhouette. Longer strokes present cleanliness and sharpness to show a tailored silhouette. Short/broken or multiple strokes create a textured, aged, ragged impression, and show a loose and shapeless silhouette (see Figure 1-80).

Figures 1-81 through 1-87 are design samples of garments with the body in action.

1-78 Garments Touching the Body

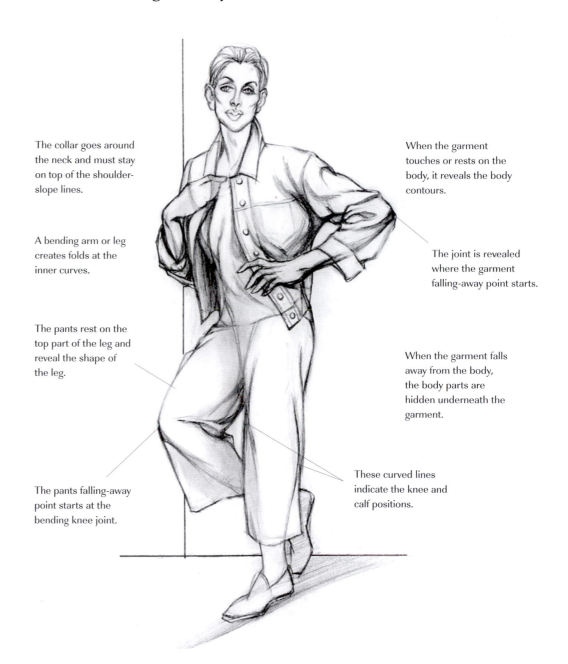

The collar goes around the neck and must stay on top of the shoulder-slope lines.

A bending arm or leg creates folds at the inner curves.

The pants rest on the top part of the leg and reveal the shape of the leg.

The pants falling-away point starts at the bending knee joint.

When the garment touches or rests on the body, it reveals the body contours.

The joint is revealed where the garment falling-away point starts.

When the garment falls away from the body, the body parts are hidden underneath the garment.

These curved lines indicate the knee and calf positions.

1-79 **Soft, Flowing Strokes**

1-80 **Short/Broken or Multiple Strokes**

1-81   **Design Sample of Garments with the Body in Action** — *Little Shop of Horrors*

Customer #1   Customer #2   Reporter   Skip Snip   Martin

LITTLE SHOP OF HORRORS
UCF Theatre Department
Summer 1999

1-82 **Design Sample of Garments with the Body in Action**—*Little Shop of Horrors*

1-83 **Design Sample of Garments with the Body in Action**—*Look Homeward, Angel*

Eliza *Act I* *Act II* *Act III*

LOOK HOMEWARD, ANGEL
UCF DEPARTMENT OF THEATRE
SPRING 2002

1-84 **Design Sample of Garments with the Body in Action—*Look Homeward, Angel***

Helen
Act I-1

Helen
Act I-2

Helen
Act III

LOOK HOMEWARD, ANGEL
UCF DEPARTMENT OF THEATRE
SPRING 2002

1-85 Design Sample of Garments with the Body in Action—*Look Homeward, Angel*

1-86 Design Sample of Garments with the Body in Action—*Look Homeward, Angel*

*Mrs. Pert
Act I-1 & 2*

*Mrs. Pert
Act II-2*

*LOOK HOMEWARD, ANGEL
UCF DEPARTMENT OF THEATRE
SPRING 2002*

*Florry Mangle
Act I & III*

*Florry Mangle
Act II*

*LOOK HOMEWARD, ANGEL
UCF DEPARTMENT OF THEATRE
SPRING 2002*

1-87   **Design Sample of Garments with the Body in Action —** *Look Homeward, Angel*

Miss Brown
Act II

Miss Brown
Act I & III

LOOK HOMEWARD, ANGEL
UCF DEPARTMENT OF THEATRE
SPRING 2002

2
Creating the Face

This chapter discusses three aspects of the face: proportions, character types, and facial expressions. Faces vary widely in shape and appearance, and they constantly appear at different angles, so there is a lot of information to learn. In costume design, figures are presented in full from head to toe. The face is only one-eighth of the whole body, but it is a very important part because it reflects personality. In my drawings and designs, I put great effort in emphasizing facial expressions as well as figure movements and actions in order to produce attitudes and personalities that create real-life characters full of vivid spirit and soul. This helps me to present my design concept, define the characters of a play, and enhance the design presentation.

Common poses include front, side, and three-quarter views, and sometimes a back view is needed. I will use these different angles to explain the basic measurements and principles of the characteristic facial expressions. The three-quarter view is the most popular and beneficial view for costume design because it is generally more descriptive and expressive than either the profile or front views. It shows a clear front view as well as a good portion of the back view while displaying a side-portion of the head and more of one cheek than the other. Also, it shows the three-dimensional masses of the brows, eyes, nose, cheeks, and jaws. The way I describe and divide the basic proportions of the face may be slightly different from the way other art books do because I use a simpler, easier method. I am going to start with the basic proportions of the face, and then get into facial expressions.

PROPORTIONS OF THE FACE—Front, Profile, and Three-Quarter Views

When drawing the front view of the face, all the features should be symmetrically balanced and proportioned. When drawing the profile view, catch the detailed curves and angles, and keep the relationships between the features connected and accurately proportioned. When drawing the three-quarter view, perspective (foreshortening) of the view will be involved. Remember, the features are placed on a round three-dimensional mass, the head. Between the front and profile views, the centerline may take an intermediate position resulting in a three-quarter view that is curved and off-center.

Step One: Establish the Head as an Abstract Form or Mass

❧ The front view of the face can be developed by using a rectangle with proportions of about 4" × 5 1/2" or 6" × 7 1/2" (see Figure 2-1).

❧ The profile of the face can be developed by using a square (see Figure 2-2).

❧ The three-quarter view of the face can be developed by using a rectangle wider than the front-view rectangle but narrower than the side-view square, about 4 1/2" × 5 1/2" or 6 1/2" × 7 1/2" (see Figure 2-3).

❧ Treat the head as an oval shape inside a block. The block will help you recognize the three-dimensional shape of heads. Think of all the features as curving around the oval block, rather than being flat. This will help you to be aware of all the planes and perspectives of the features when drawing the head.

❧ Draw oval shapes in the front, profile, and three-quarter views for the basic head forms (see Figures 2-4 through 2-6). The oval in the profile view is placed from corner to corner in any direction. The oval in the three-quarter view can be placed in either direction.

2-1 Rectangle for Front View

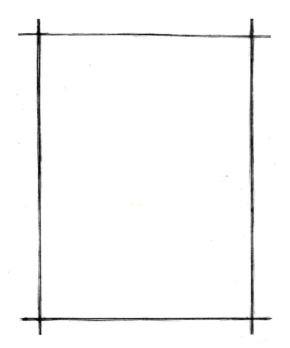

2-2 Square for Profile View

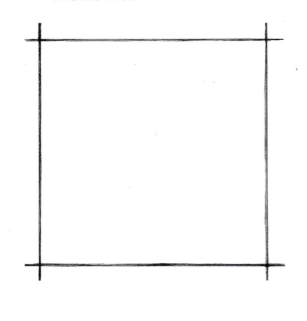

2-3 Rectangle for Three-Quarter View

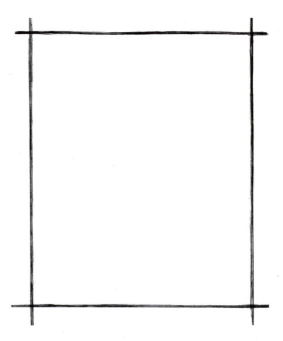

2-4 **Placement of Oval Shape inside Front View Rectangle**

2-5 **Placement of Oval Shape inside Profile View Square**

2-6 **Placement of Oval Shape inside Three-Quarter View Rectangle**

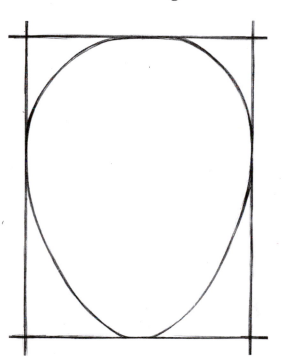

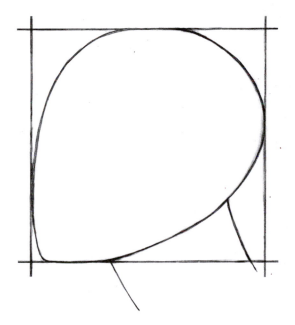

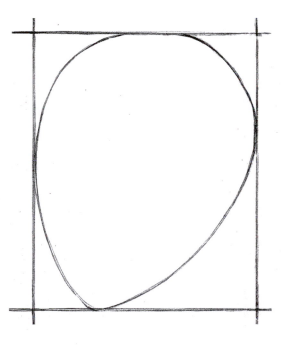

Step Two: Block in the Features

The primary placement of the features determines the unique appearance of the face. When drawing a full figure, it is important to catch and emphasize the action lines; when drawing a face, capture the mood of the character and put particular feature changes in the right place to make them stand out.

It is very important when developing a face to first block all the features, rather than drawing them one at a time. If the features are drawn separately, the result is often lopsided and unbalanced. Each individual feature may look perfectly fine, but when looking at the features as a whole, they are out of proportion. You must consider the features in relation to one another and establish the correct proportions to produce a balanced, realistic face. The placement of the features for front, profile, and three-quarter views is determined by the same rules, but the centerline in the profile and three-quarter views becomes curved.

❦ To establish the placement of the features for the front view, draw a centerline running vertically inside the block. This will be the center of the face (see Figure 2-7). The centerline will be between the eyes and will divide the nose and mouth into equal halves. When the head moves to different views, the centerline moves as well. Thus, the centerline of the profile will be at the edge of the profile block (see Figure 2-8). In the three-quarter view, the centerline moves to either side of the block, depending on which way the head turns (see Figure 2-9). When facing left, the centerline moves to the left; when facing right, the centerline moves to the right. The centerline is curved, whether the head is facing left or right.

❦ Draw horizontal lines inside each of the three oval shapes to indicate the placement of the eyes. The eyes are located halfway between the top of the head and the bottom of the chin (see Figures 2-10 through 2-12).

2-7 Placement of the Centerline for Front View

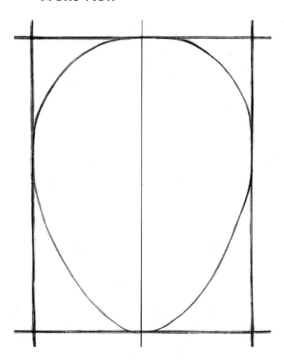

2-8 Placement of the Centerline for Profile View

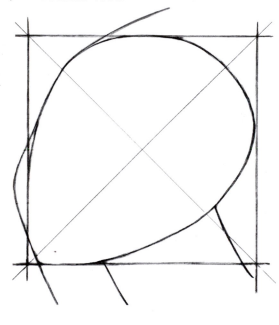

2-9 Placement of the Centerline for Three-Quarter View

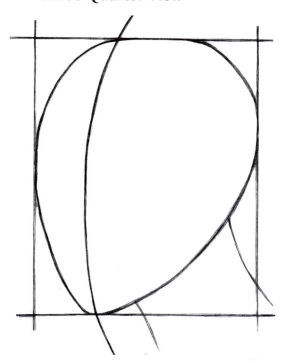

🔖 In the front view (Figure 2-10), divide the length of the horizontal line into five equal parts. One part equals the length of an eye. The distance between the two eyes equals one eye.

🔖 In the profile view (Figure 2-11), draw diagonal lines running from corner to corner inside the square to establish the hairline and the top of the ear where it connects to the face.

🔖 The nose is vertically set at the center of the face. Draw a horizontal line halfway between the eyes and chin to indicate the bottom of the nose. The width of the nose is a little bit wider than the distance between the two eyes.

🔖 Draw a horizontal line one third of the way down from the bottom of the nose to the chin to indicate the opening of the mouth. The width of the mouth is a little wider than the width of the nose.

🔖 The top edge of the ear lines up with the eyebrow; the bottom of the ear lines up with the bottom of the nose.

🔖 The distance from the hairline to the eyebrows will be about equal to the distance from the bottom of the nose to the eyebrows.

🔖 Add eyebrows above the eyes, according to the shape of the eyes.

🔖 As the head turns or tilts, the lines will change shape, direction, and position. As the head changes position, the distance between these lines will change, but they will still remain parallel to one another.

2-10 Placement of Features in Front View

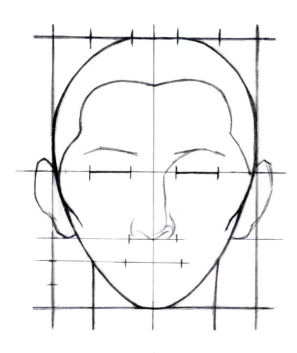

2-11 Placement of Features in Profile View

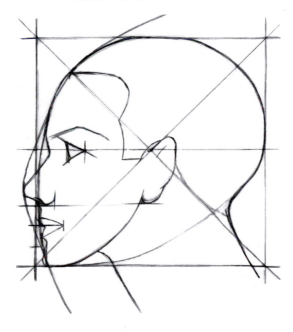

2-12 Placement of Features in Three-Quarter View

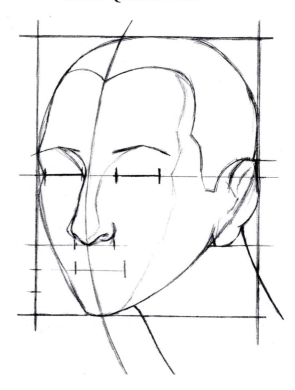

Step Three: Contour the Features

Contouring Eyes and Eyebrows (see Figure 2-13)

- The eye is formed around a sphere-shaped setting in the eye socket. The eyelids are wrapped around the eyeball in a curve that shows the contour of the three-dimensional eyeball.

- The upper eyelids look darker and thicker than the bottom eyelids because of the eyelashes and cast shadows. Following the shape of the upper eyelids, draw a curved line to create a double eyelid.

- The side view of the eye is a curved line formed around the eyeball.

- The three-quarter view of the eye will have a perspective aspect. The eye that is turned away should be slightly smaller than the closer eye.

- The iris is a perfect circle, but the top of the iris is partially covered by the upper eyelid when motionless. You should never color the iris in solid because that will cause the eye to lose its life and sparkle. The eyes mirror emotions and moods and are the windows to the spirit of the soul. They are crystal-like; highlighted spots are always favorable.

- Eyelashes are not all the same length. The inner part of the eyelashes is shorter than the outer corners. They grow along the eyelids, curved up on the top eyelid, and curved down at the lower eyelid.

- Eyebrows protect and grow above the eyes. Eyebrow shape follows the shape of the eye. The middle part of the eyebrow is thicker and darker than the ends because the eyebrows overlap together. Don't draw the eyebrow as a solid thick line.

2-13 Contouring Eyes and Eyebrows

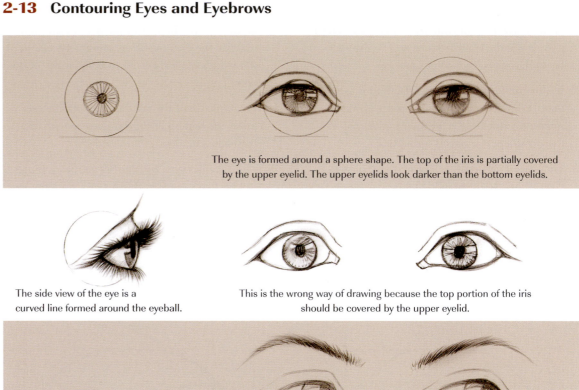

The eye is formed around a sphere shape. The top of the iris is partially covered by the upper eyelid. The upper eyelids look darker than the bottom eyelids.

The side view of the eye is a curved line formed around the eyeball.

This is the wrong way of drawing because the top portion of the iris should be covered by the upper eyelid.

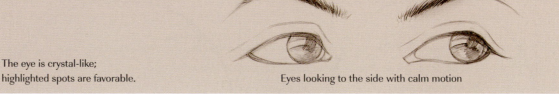

The eye is crystal-like; highlighted spots are favorable.

Eyes looking to the side with calm motion

Eyelashes are curved, growing along the eyelids.

Eyes looking down to side with fearful expression

The inner part of the eyelashes is shorter than the outer corners.

Correct way of drawing eyelashes

Wrong way of drawing eyelashes

Contouring the Nose (see Figure 2-14)

❧ The nose is symmetrically set in the center of the face. There are four basic planes that structure nose shape—the top, the two sides, and the bottom. It is narrower at the top and wider near the bottom. The profile of the nose is easiest to draw, whereas the frontal view is most difficult. The three-quarter view of the nose usually overlaps with the corner of the eye farthest away. Only three planes of the nose are visible in the three-quarter view. Angular and straight lines should be used for the middle of the nose bridge; curved and less angular lines should be used for the bottom of the nose. Applying some shadows around the nose bridge will help to define the shape.

Contouring Ears (see Figure 2-14)

❧ Keep the ears simple. They should never be the prominent feature. The ears stand out from the side of the head and slant back at an angle. The top edge of the ear lines up with the eyebrow; the bottom of the ear lines up with the bottom of the nose and merges with the jawline. Contour lines of the ear overlap one another. Some lines overlap in the front, and some lines stay behind to show the particular curves and shapes of the ear.

Contouring the Mouth (see Figure 2-14)

❧ The mouth displays a large amount of emotional expression. The degree of change can be from subtle to extreme. The upper and lower lips are different in shape. The shape of the upper lip is usually sharper, thinner, more curved, and darker because of the shadow cast from natural light; the bottom lip is usually fuller, rounder, and lighter toned. The three-quarter view of the lip should have perspective aspect.

2-14 Contouring the Nose, Ear, and Mouth

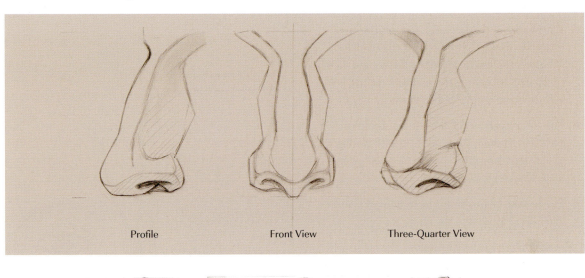

Profile   Front View   Three-Quarter View

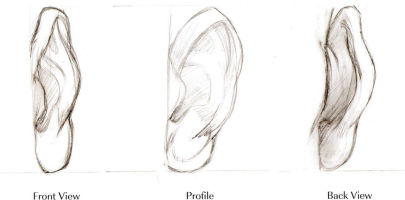

Front View   Profile   Back View

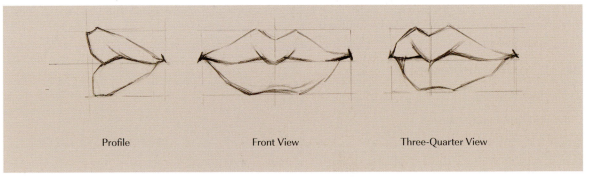

Profile   Front View   Three-Quarter View

Contouring the Outline of the Face (see Figures 2-15 through 2-20)

🦋 The shapes of the forehead and hairline are related to each other because if the hairline is higher, the forehead will be larger, and vice versa. The hair along the temple has little peaks, and the temple area slightly dents in.

🦋 The widest part of the face is the cheekbone area. The contour lines of the cheek overlap with the jawline, since the cheeks are more prominent than the jaws.

🦋 The jawline begins from the bottom of the ear and curves around to the chin.

Contouring the male face follows the same principles as contouring the female face except the contour lines on the male face are more angular and firm. The differences between the male and female face include the following:

Face:

M: egg- or rectangular-shaped with an angular jawline

F: egg-shaped with a pointed chin and a smooth, curved jawline

Eyebrows:

M: natural, usually thicker and angular in shape

F: fine and curved, usually plucked or outlined with makeup

Space between the eyebrow and eye:

M: narrow space

F: wider and more spacious

2-15   Contouring the Head and Facial Features; Front View, Female

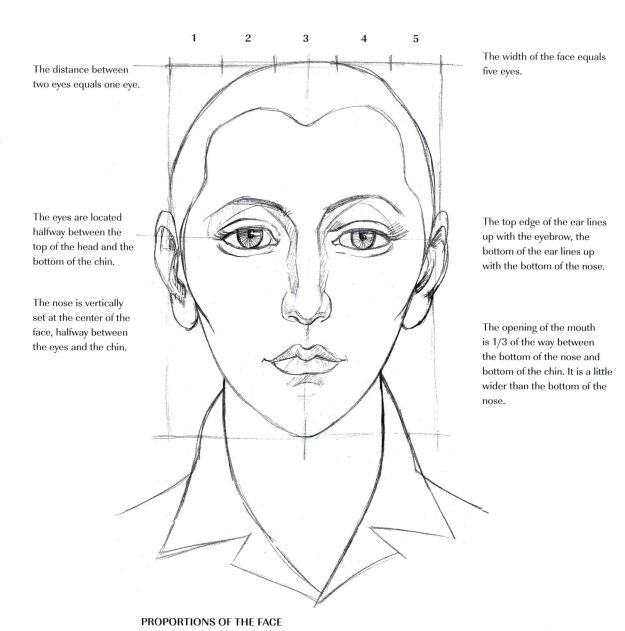

The distance between two eyes equals one eye.

The eyes are located halfway between the top of the head and the bottom of the chin.

The nose is vertically set at the center of the face, halfway between the eyes and the chin.

The width of the face equals five eyes.

The top edge of the ear lines up with the eyebrow, the bottom of the ear lines up with the bottom of the nose.

The opening of the mouth is 1/3 of the way between the bottom of the nose and bottom of the chin. It is a little wider than the bottom of the nose.

PROPORTIONS OF THE FACE

Nose:

M: angular with a well-defined nose bridge and nostrils

F: well-defined with soft curves

Lips:

M: well-defined, thick and angular

F: well-defined with soft curves

Neck:

M: thick and muscular, more skeletal, shows two sternocleidomastoideus muscles, neck outline usually starts between outer corner of eye and outline of side face, noticeable throat bones

F: thin and smooth, outline of neck usually lines up with outer corner of eye, throat bones are less visible, the sternocleidomastoid muscles much smoother

2-16 Contouring the Head and Facial Features; Profile View, Female

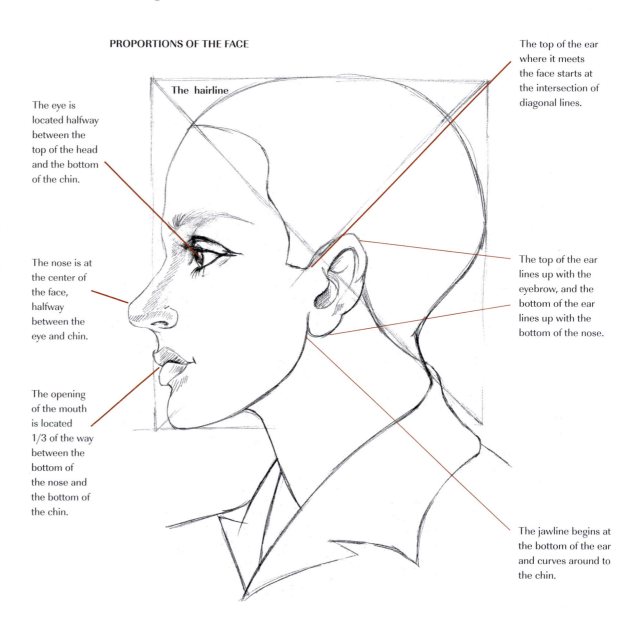

PROPORTIONS OF THE FACE

The hairline

The eye is located halfway between the top of the head and the bottom of the chin.

The nose is at the center of the face, halfway between the eye and chin.

The opening of the mouth is located 1/3 of the way between the bottom of the nose and the bottom of the chin.

The top of the ear where it meets the face starts at the intersection of diagonal lines.

The top of the ear lines up with the eyebrow, and the bottom of the ear lines up with the bottom of the nose.

The jawline begins at the bottom of the ear and curves around to the chin.

2-17 Contouring the Head and Facial Features; Three-Quarter View, Female

PROPORTIONS OF THE FACE

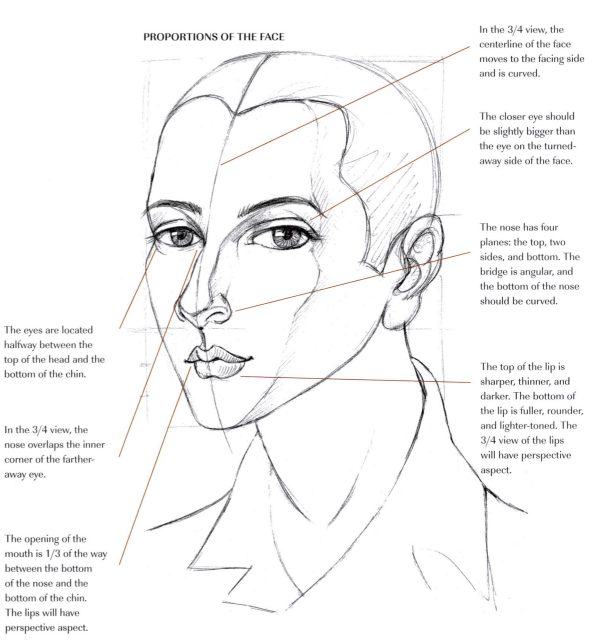

In the 3/4 view, the centerline of the face moves to the facing side and is curved.

The closer eye should be slightly bigger than the eye on the turned-away side of the face.

The nose has four planes: the top, two sides, and bottom. The bridge is angular, and the bottom of the nose should be curved.

The top of the lip is sharper, thinner, and darker. The bottom of the lip is fuller, rounder, and lighter-toned. The 3/4 view of the lips will have perspective aspect.

The eyes are located halfway between the top of the head and the bottom of the chin.

In the 3/4 view, the nose overlaps the inner corner of the farther-away eye.

The opening of the mouth is 1/3 of the way between the bottom of the nose and the bottom of the chin. The lips will have perspective aspect.

2-18 **Contouring the Head and Facial Features; Front View, Male**

PROPORTIONS OF THE FACE

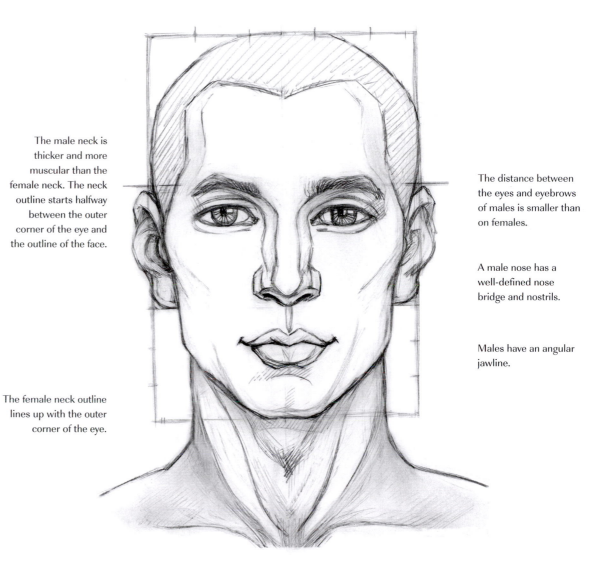

The male neck is thicker and more muscular than the female neck. The neck outline starts halfway between the outer corner of the eye and the outline of the face.

The female neck outline lines up with the outer corner of the eye.

The distance between the eyes and eyebrows of males is smaller than on females.

A male nose has a well-defined nose bridge and nostrils.

Males have an angular jawline.

2-19 **Contouring the Head and Facial Features; Profile View, Male**

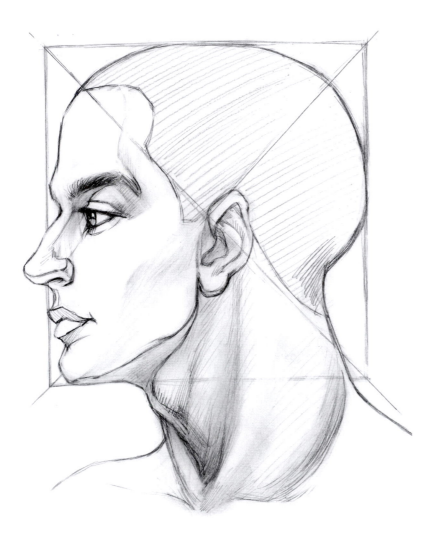

2-20 **Contouring the Head and Facial Features; Three-Quarter View, Male**

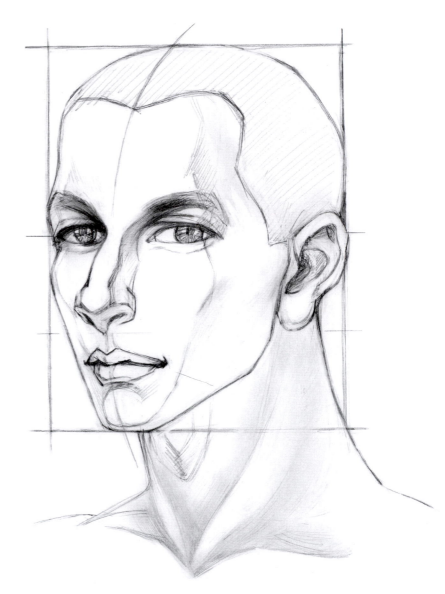

Create shadows and reflecting lights to emphasize the three-dimensional structures of the bottom of the nose and chin. Cheekbones can be defined by subtle shadows, but do not over-stress them.

The positions of facial features are associated with the turning of the head and face. We discussed the relationships between the head, chest, and pelvis masses in Chapter 1. We also discussed how the arms and chest move as one unit, and how the legs and pelvis move as the other unit. Among these masses, the head is most visible. The head, face, and facial features are also related to one another as a unit. When the head turns or tilts in a certain direction, the facial features will follow. The head and face have subtle planes in a three-dimensional egg-shaped form. All the features sit on an egg-shaped curved surface, not a two-dimensional flat surface. When the head is in a straight position, the centerline of the face is straight and all the features are lined up with horizontal lines, as explained earlier. When the head turns up or down, or left or right, the horizontal lines curve (see Figures 2-21 and 2-22). If the head turns up, larger portions of the bottom of the nose, lip, and chin will show, compared to the top. Also, the distance between the features shortens as the head turns. The same philosophy occurs when the head turns down (more of the top of the head, forehead, nose bridge, cheeks, lips, and chin will be seen). The amount of top and bottom portions of each feature seen is based on the degree that the head turns. If you block all features together, situate them in relation to one another first, balance the proportions of the features, and remember that the face is not a flat surface, you will not make mistakes when drawing a face.

2-21 **Head in Different Positions**

HEAD LOOKING DOWN

When the head turns down, more of the top of the head, forehead, nose bridge, cheeks, bottom lip, and chin will be seen.

When the head turns up, down, or to the side, the facial features line up with these curves and are parallel.

HEAD LOOKING UP

The distance between the features is shortened.

When the head turns up, more of the lower portions of the nose, lips, and chin will be seen.

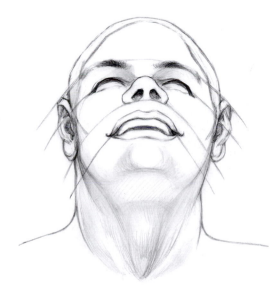

2-22 Head in Different Positions

HEAD TURNED TO THE SIDE

The head, face, and facial features are related to one another.

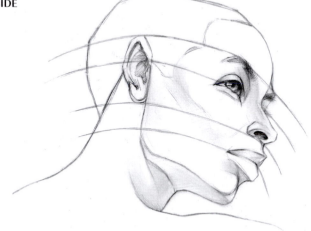

When the head turns or tilts in a certain direction, the facial features will follow as a unit. All the features line up on curved lines.

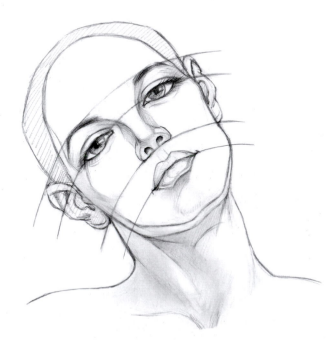

TYPES AND CHARACTERISTICS OF FACES

Clearly, the face is an important part of the human body—it identifies who you are, conveys emotions, and exhibits new fashions in current hairstyles and makeup. Today, especially in the United States, there is a diverse society. Theatre productions, films, television shows, and the fine arts strongly reflect this multicultural uniqueness—a globalized universe requires the ability to draw different facial features and body types. A costume designer should not only portray the beauty of the costume, but should also be capable of creating a figure of any ethnicity.

Every race has a distinct and unique face. The following discussion is based on my studies and observations of faces through living abroad, watching movies and television, and interacting with people from different cultures. Living in the United States actually has helped me to understand my own culture better. This opportunity shaped and inspired me to create my own unique characterization of design.

If you use the profile view to start the four face types, you will immediately notice the differences between them. Use a vertical line as a guideline. In Caucasian profiles, the forehead, lips, and chin line up in a vertical line. In African profiles, the vertical line is at an angle because of the forward

jawlines. The Asian profile line angle is between the Caucasian's and African's line. In Middle Eastern profiles, facial features line up the same as they do in Caucasian profiles, except Middle Eastern faces have larger features and thicker facial hair. The vertical line is used as a drawing guide, but adjustments will be made when the face is tilted or in up or down positions.

As examples, I discuss four major ethnic groups (see Tables 2-1 through 2-4).

2-23 Characteristics of Faces

Face profiles have different angles.

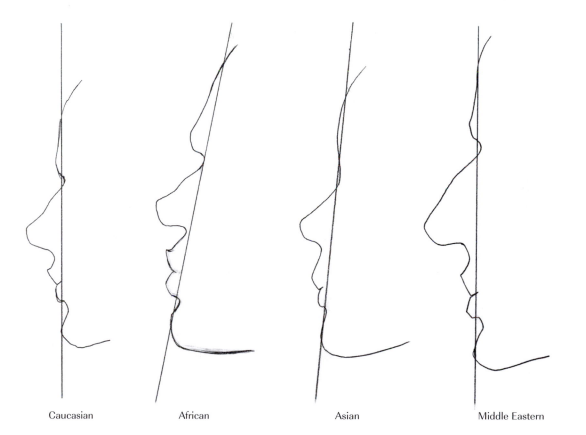

Caucasian   African   Asian   Middle Eastern

Table 2-1	Characteristics of Caucasian Faces (see Figures 2-24 through 2-26)
Face shape	Egg- or oval-shaped
Face color	Pinkish or white
Eyebrow texture	Medium thick and well defined
Eyebrow color	Black, shades of brown, red, and blonde
Eye shape	Large with a double eyelid and long eyelashes; deep eye socket
Eye color	Black, dark brown, brown, blue, green, or hazel
Nose shape	Long and straight with a high nose bridge
Lip shape	Well defined; generally small and thin
Lip color	Red or pinkish
Hair	Wavy or straight, fine, colored

2-24 Characteristics of a Caucasian Face, Female Profile

In a Caucasian profile, the forehead, lips, and chin line up vertically.

2-25 Characteristics of a Caucasian Face, Male Front View

Well-defined features, deep eye sockets

2-26 Characteristics of a Caucasian Face, Male Three-Quarter View

Deep eye sockets, a long, straight, and high nose bridge, thin and small lips

Table 2-2 Characteristics of African Faces (see Figures 2-27 through 2-29)	
Face shape	Egg-, oval-, or rectangular-shaped
Face color	Dark, dark brown, brown, or light brown
Eyebrow texture	Medium thick and well defined
Eyebrow color	Black, dark brown, brown
Eye shape	Large with double eyelid and long eyelashes; deep eye socket
Eye color	Black, shades of brown
Nose shape	Angular or curvy with an elevated nose bridge; wider nostrils
Lip shape	Well defined; thick and luscious; jaw is forward
Lip color	Darker color in upper lip, red or reddish brown in lower lip
Hair color	Black or dark brown
Hair type	Thick; small and tight curves, medium thick facial hair

2-27 Characteristics of an African Face, Male Profile

In an African profile, the forehead and jawline form a slanted line.

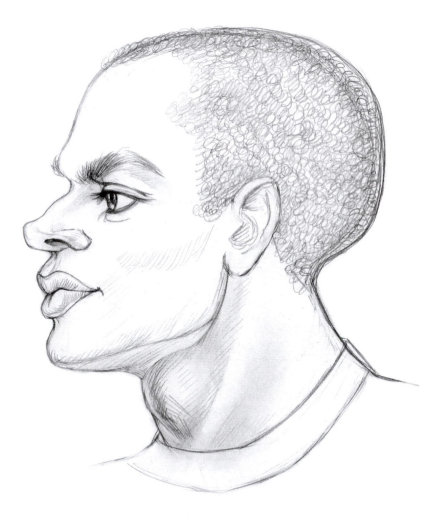

2-28 Characteristics of an African Face, Female Front View

Africans have big eyes, deep eye sockets, and full lips.

2-29 Characteristics of an African Face, Male Three-Quarter View

Africans have full lips, angular noses with an elevated nose bridge, wider nostrils, and forward jawlines.

Table 2-3 Characteristics of Asian Faces (see Figures 2-30 through 2-32)	
Face shape	Egg-, square-, rectangular-shaped, or round; wide and flat
Face color	Light brown, yellow, shades of tan
Eyebrow texture	Fine and well defined
Eyebrow color	Black, shades of brown
Eye shape	Small, narrow, and slanting upward at the outer corner; thin and short eyelashes; single or small double eyelid and shallow eye socket
Eye color	Black, shades of brown; small iris
Nose shape	Generally short; lower nose bridge
Lip shape	Well defined, medium thick (thicker than Caucasian's and thinner than African's); jaws are forward
Lip color	Red, pinkish, brown
Hair type	Black, dark brown, thick/thin and straight; very thin facial hair

2-30 Characteristics of an Asian Face, Female Profile

In an Asian profile, the upper and lower jaws are forward.

2-31 **Characteristics of an Asian Face, Female Front View**

Asians have a wide and flatter facial structure, flatter eye sockets, lower nose bridge, and small eyes with small double eyelids.

2-32 **Characteristics of an Asian Face, Male Three-Quarter View**

Asians have square-shaped faces, shorter noses, wider cheekbones, slightly forward jaws, and narrow eyes slanting upward at the outer corners.

Table 2-4	Characteristics of Middle Eastern Faces (see Figures 2-33 through 2-35)
Face shape	Egg-, oval-, or rectangular-shaped
Face color	Olive or tan
Eyebrow texture	Thick and well defined in shape
Eyebrow color	Black, dark brown
Eye shape	Big; double eyelid with thick and long eyelashes; deep eye socket
Eye color	Black, shades of brown
Nose shape	Long, straight, and high nose bridge
Lip shape	Well defined, medium thick
Lip color	Red or pinkish
Hair type	Black or dark brown; wavy; very thick facial hair

2-33 Characteristics of a Middle Eastern Face, Male Profile

In a Middle Eastern profile, the forehead, lips, and chin line up vertically as they do in Caucasian faces, except Middle Eastern faces have larger features and thicker facial hair.

2-34 Characteristics of a Middle Eastern Face, Male Front View

Middle Eastern people have larger facial features, thick and dark facial hair, and high and straight nose bridges.

2-35 Characteristics of a Middle Eastern Face, Female Three-Quarter View

Middle Eastern people have well-defined facial features; their facial features are slightly larger than Caucasians'; they have big eyes, thicker eyebrows, and fuller lips.

FACIAL EXPRESSIONS

Facial expressions in art have always amazed me and attracted my attention. When I look at a painting of a deeply emotional character, I feel like I am inside the character's soul. I studied Gary Faigin's book, *The Artist's Complete Guide to Facial Expression,* which is an excellent reference for any costume designer. It helped me to understand facial movements and how the facial muscles function during a particular emotion. I also find Norman Rockwell's paintings fascinating, and I greatly admire his work. All his characters are alive and tell stories. The viewer is able to look into their souls and relate to their feelings. I can spend hours looking at his paintings, studying how he portrays his characters and what specific details he used to capture the spirit of the people in his paintings. I am always encouraged and inspired by these works of masters. Facial expressions are important to my costume designs because they create a unique expression that shows the character's feelings, emotions, and demeanor. They distinguish the character's age, sex, occupation, status, personality, nationality, and so on. Facial expression and body language enhance individuality and portray realistic people with developed personalities.

Design or creative artwork has a wide diversity of styles just like cooking. When you add spices to food, you create a special flavor. If you don't add spice to your food, the taste will be bland and plain. When you draw a figure without defined facial features, the figure looks like a mannequin. When you add facial features to the face, the figure will look like a human being and will come to life. The facial expression is equally significant to the costume in portraying the character's mood, personality, occupation, age, gender, and so on.

How Can Proper Facial Expression Be Achieved?

When creating facial expressions, you should feel comfortable and do it with interest so that you do it well. A positive attitude must be the starting point.

Traditionally, most drawing books show facial movements and expressions from the bone structure to the musculature. Then they show how the muscles relate to bone structure and how the muscles move the surface of the face to create facial expressions.

Most of the drawings I present show the visible surface of the face. I will not discuss the deep layers of muscles and bones at this time but the subject is important because the deep layers will help you to understand how the surface of the face moves. I will focus only on the surface for simplicity.

Emotions

A person's moods and actions direct their expressions or movements of features. Those movements are revealed on the surface of the face and occur the same way in any human race, sex, age, or nationality group. The brain controls emotions; the emotions change the forms of the features. The eyes are the windows to the soul; they mirror the emotions and moods of the character. When a character is laughing, the eyes are narrowed and wrinkled at the outer corners. Anger, pleasure, sadness, and joy are reflected in the eyes, nostrils, mouth, cheeks, and jaws. When facial features are affected by emotions, they are each directly affected, but they also collaborate and affect each other as a team. When you create a facial expression, imagine all the features moving with one another to form that expression. If you change just one feature for an expression, you will not capture true emotions, just false ones. Working all the features as a whole is important.

Again, drawing is like cooking. A spicy flavor may not suit everyone's taste, but it creates a different flavor. In art, the special flavor is a unique style. Sometimes I spend more time on facial features and their expressions than on other parts of the body. I strictly demand that from myself be-

cause I consider it an important part of the creative work that completes my costume design. Putting more time into the facial expressions may not work for everybody. Just like a food preference where some people like a spicy taste while others may like a sweeter or more sour flavor, each artist should develop his or her own style and preference in expressing himself or herself.

I categorize four major facial expressions that are often used for costume design figures:

🐚 Happy/Smiling/Laughing

🐚 Sad/Crying/Depressed

🐚 Angry/Shouting/Hatred

🐚 Surprised/Fear/Frightened

These four major expressions can be demonstrated with the simple abstract forms in Figures 2-36 through 2-39.

2-36 Abstract Form of Happy/Smiling/Laughing

2-37 Abstract Form of Sad/Crying/Depressed

2-38 Abstract Form of Angry/Shouting/Hatred

2-39 Abstract Form of Surprised/Fear/Frightened

HAPPY/SMILING/LAUGHING

When a person is smiling or laughing, keep the following in mind (see Figures 2-40 through 2-47).

- Muscles of the face are stretched or spread outward from the center of the face.

- Eyebrows are relaxed and slightly raised.

- Eyes will narrow and curve up in a crescent shape. The outer corner of the eyes may have some crow's-feet. When a person is smiling, the lower eyelid will rise up and cover the lower part of the iris.

- Nostrils will be pulled up, which develops laugh lines along them. Cheeks are pushed up.

- Cheeks are raised and round like an apple. The shape and position of cheekbones are basically defined by laugh lines, subtle lights, and shadows. Shadows faintly appear, but are not overdone.

- Corners of the mouth rise upward and the mouth widens, opens, and usually shows upper teeth. Lower teeth may not be seen or are seen only slightly. Both the upper and lower lips stretch tightly around the teeth and jaws.

- Lower jaw drops. The bigger the open mouth, the lower the jaw will drop.

- The mouth can be difficult to draw. It can easily change in shape and appearance. Even a slight downward or upward modification around the corners will alter the character's entire emotional presence. Degree of change can also affect the shape and size of the lips.

- Be aware that hair grows above the skull and has fullness. Do not draw hair as if it is painted on the skull.

2-40 Happy/Smiling/Laughing Expression, Front View

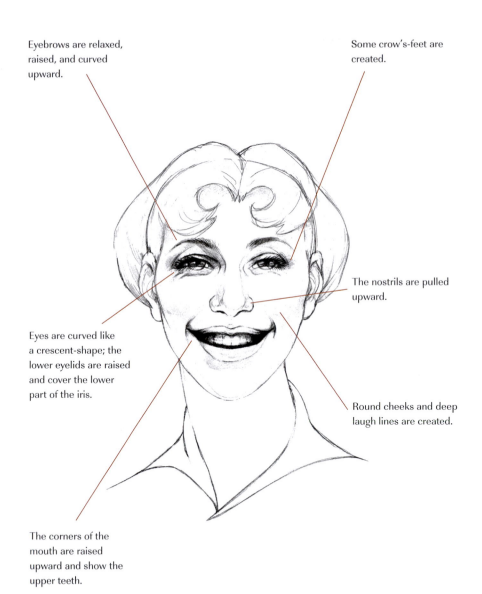

Eyebrows are relaxed, raised, and curved upward.

Some crow's-feet are created.

The nostrils are pulled upward.

Eyes are curved like a crescent-shape; the lower eyelids are raised and cover the lower part of the iris.

Round cheeks and deep laugh lines are created.

The corners of the mouth are raised upward and show the upper teeth.

2-41 Happy/Smiling/Laughing Expression, Profile View

The hair grows above the skull.

The eyebrow is relaxed, raised, and curved.

The eye is curved in a crescent shape; the lower eyelid raises up. Both the top and bottom of the iris are covered by the upper and lower eyelids. Some crow's feet are created.

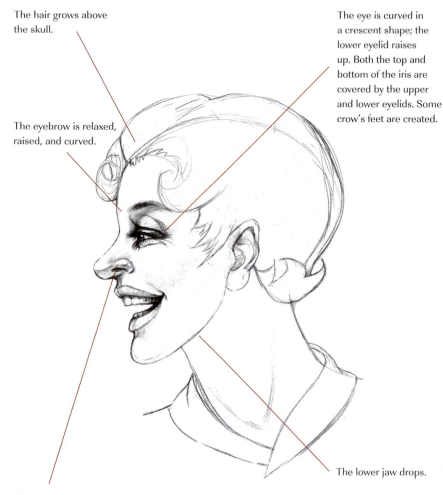

The nostril is pulled upward, creating a round cheek and laugh line, sometimes showing both the top and bottom teeth.

The lower jaw drops.

2-42 Happy/Smiling/Laughing Expression, Three-Quarter View

Eyebrows are raised, curved, and relaxed.

The nostrils are pulled upward, and deep laugh lines and round cheeks are created.

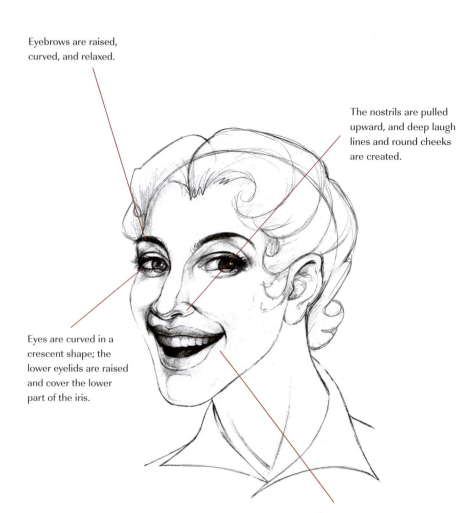

Eyes are curved in a crescent shape; the lower eyelids are raised and cover the lower part of the iris.

The corners of the mouth are raised upward and show the upper teeth.

2-43   **Design Sample of Happy Expression—**
The Butterfingers Angel

2-44   **Design Sample of Happy Expression—**
Big River

2-45 **Design Sample of Happy Expression—*Big River***

BIG RIVER
UCF THEATRE
Spring 1999

2-46 Design Sample of Happy Expression—
Run for Your Wife

2-47 Design Sample of Happy Expression—
Look Homeward Angel

SAD/CRYING/DEPRESSED

The movements of the features of a sad person are in the opposite direction of a happy person. All the lines are downward. See Figures 2-48 through 2-53.

🙢 Inner corners of the eyes and eyebrows pull upward together, and lower corners drop down. This will create some vertical lines between the eyebrows.

🙢 Eyes tend to be closed or half-closed and show frowns. The upper and lower eyelids cover both the top and bottom of the iris.

🙢 Nostrils tend to open wide and stretch to the side, sometimes creating downward deep folds along the nostrils.

🙢 Corners of the mouth will drop. If the mouth closes, it will squeeze tight. If the mouth opens, the upper lip usually covers the upper teeth. Lower teeth are sometimes shown.

🙢 Lower jaw drops to some degree.

🙢 Hair grows from the skull and should be above it and have fullness.

2-48 Sad/Crying/Depressed Expression, Front View

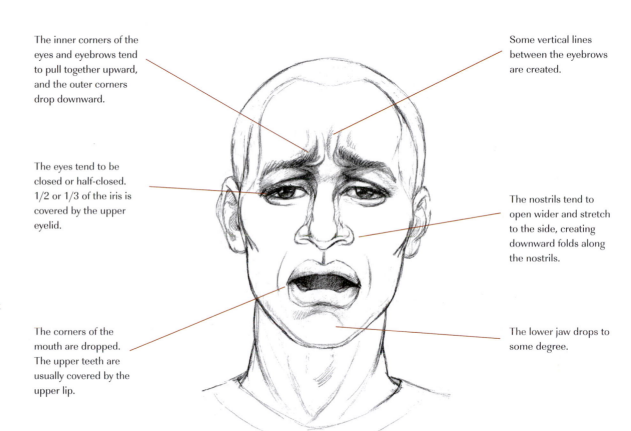

The inner corners of the eyes and eyebrows tend to pull together upward, and the outer corners drop downward.

The eyes tend to be closed or half-closed. 1/2 or 1/3 of the iris is covered by the upper eyelid.

The corners of the mouth are dropped. The upper teeth are usually covered by the upper lip.

Some vertical lines between the eyebrows are created.

The nostrils tend to open wider and stretch to the side, creating downward folds along the nostrils.

The lower jaw drops to some degree.

2-49 Sad/Crying/Depressed Expression, Profile View

2-50 Sad/Crying/Depressed Expression, Three-Quarter View

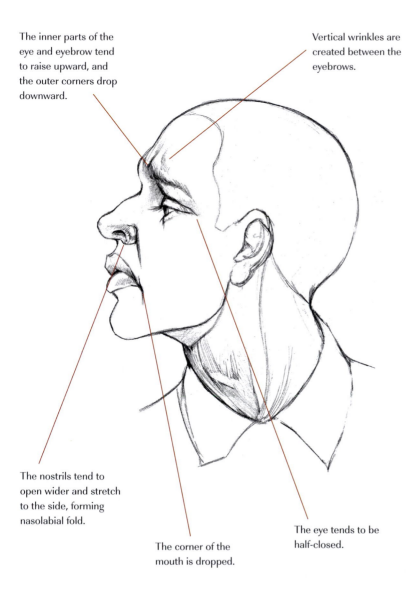

The inner parts of the eye and eyebrow tend to raise upward, and the outer corners drop downward.

Vertical wrinkles are created between the eyebrows.

The nostrils tend to open wider and stretch to the side, forming nasolabial fold.

The corner of the mouth is dropped.

The eye tends to be half-closed.

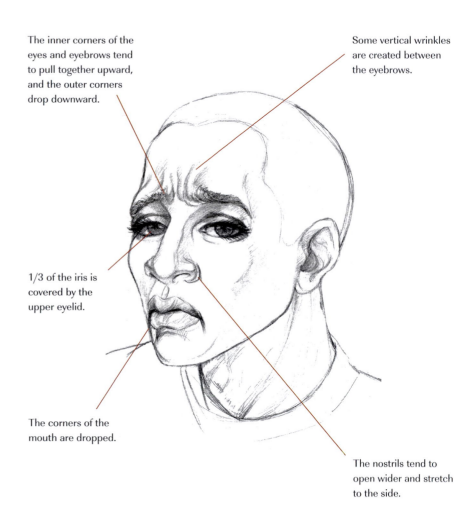

The inner corners of the eyes and eyebrows tend to pull together upward, and the outer corners drop downward.

Some vertical wrinkles are created between the eyebrows.

1/3 of the iris is covered by the upper eyelid.

The corners of the mouth are dropped.

The nostrils tend to open wider and stretch to the side.

2-51 **Design Sample of Sad Expression—**
Death of a Salesman

DEATH OF A SALESMAN
UCF THEATRE SPRING 2002

WILLY
ACT I

WILLY ACT I

WILLY
ACT II

2-52 **Design Sample of Sad Expression—**
Death of a Salesman

DEATH OF A SALESMAN
UCF THEATRE SPRING 2002

LINDA
ACT I

LINDA
ACT II

LINDA
ACT II

2-53   Design Sample of Sad Expression—*Little Shop of Horrors*

ANGRY/SHOUTING/HATRED

When people get mad, their features create intense and angular shapes. See Figures 2-54 through 2-58.

୫ Inner corners of the eyebrows pull downward and toward the center of the face, close to the inner corners of the eyes. Back of the eyebrows stand up to form angular peaks.

୫ Eyes are more square-shaped and widely opened. The iris seems to be ready to fall out of the eye socket, and the top edge of the iris is exposed. Space between the eyebrows and eyes diminishes, showing vertical wrinkles.

୫ Nostrils rise and open widely, forming deep, sharp, downward nasolabial folds.

୫ Mouth is square-shaped, widely open, and shows both the upper and lower teeth. The wider the mouth, the more extreme the shouting.

2-54 Angry/Shouting/Hatred Expression, Front View

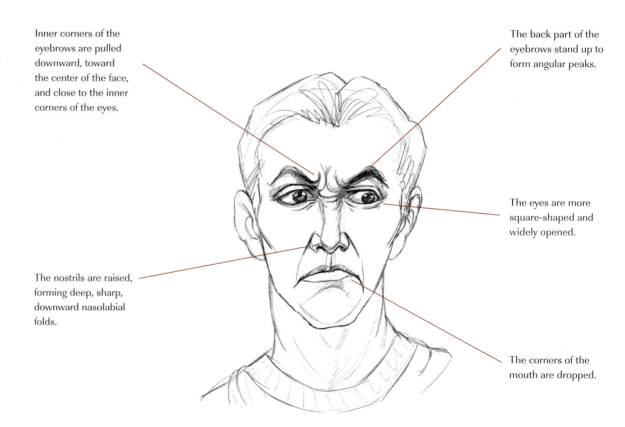

Inner corners of the eyebrows are pulled downward, toward the center of the face, and close to the inner corners of the eyes.

The back part of the eyebrows stand up to form angular peaks.

The eyes are more square-shaped and widely opened.

The nostrils are raised, forming deep, sharp, downward nasolabial folds.

The corners of the mouth are dropped.

2-55 Angry/Shouting/Hatred Expression, Profile View

2-56 Angry/Shouting/Hatred Expression, Three-Quarter View

The inner part of the eyebrow is pulled downward and toward the center of the face. There are some vertical wrinkles between the eyebrows.

The back part of the eyebrow stands up to form an angular peak.

The inner corners of the eyebrows are pulled downward and toward the center of the face.

The back parts of the eyebrows stand up to form angular peaks.

The eye becomes square-shaped and widely opened.

The nostrils are raised and widely opened, forming deep, downward nasolabial folds.

The eyes are square-shaped and widely opened, showing the top edge of the iris.

The nostril is raised, forming a deep nasolabial fold.

The mouth becomes square-shaped and widely opened, showing both the upper and lower teeth.

The wider the mouth is open, the more extreme the shouting.

The mouth is square, widely open and showing both the upper and lower teeth. The lower jaw is dropped.

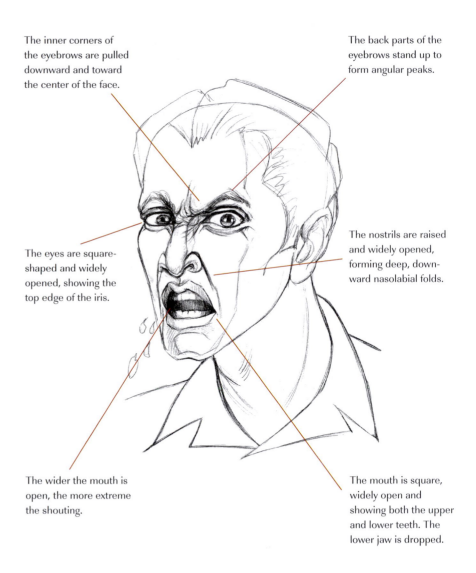

2-57   Design Sample of Angry Expression—*Crazy for You*

2-58   **Design Sample of Angry Expression—*Little Shop of Horrors***

SURPRISED/FEAR/FRIGHTENED

Surprise, fear, and fright have common characteristics (see Figures 2-59 through 2-63):

- Forehead wrinkles are developed.

- Eyebrows lift upward as far as possible.

- Eyes open as wide as possible.

- White part of the eye shows the most.

- Whole circle of the iris is exposed.

- Mouth opens widely and downward with tension. When the person is in fear, sometimes the lower teeth are visible.

- Mouth opens in an oval or circle when the person has a very surprised look. Also, lips are relaxed and teeth are hidden.

- Mouth is closed together and pulled forward when person is slightly and pleasantly surprised.

- Lower jaw drops in proportion to the opening of the mouth.

2-59 Surprised/Fear/Frightened Expression, Front View

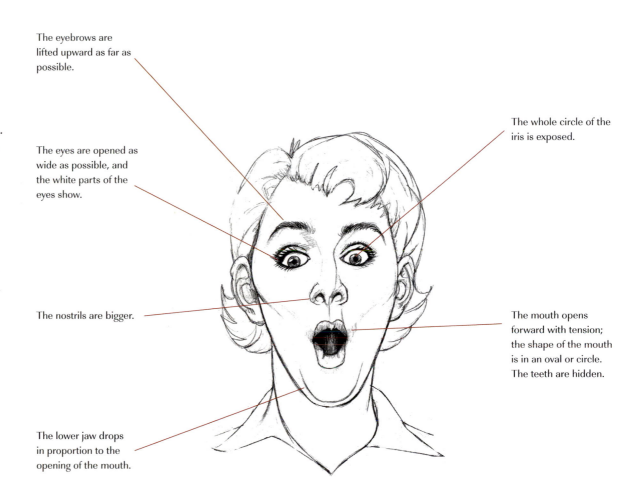

The eyebrows are lifted upward as far as possible.

The eyes are opened as wide as possible, and the white parts of the eyes show.

The nostrils are bigger.

The lower jaw drops in proportion to the opening of the mouth.

The whole circle of the iris is exposed.

The mouth opens forward with tension; the shape of the mouth is in an oval or circle. The teeth are hidden.

2-60 Surprised/Fear/Frightened Expression, Profile View

The hair grows above the skull.

The side view of the eye should be treated as curved lines formed around the eyeball, and only half of the eye is shown.

The eyebrow lifts upward as far as possible.

The eye opens as wide as possible, and the white part of the eye shows.

The mouth is widely opened, and the lower jaw is dropped in proportion to the opening of the mouth.

The lips are relaxed and cover both the top and bottom teeth.

2-61 Surprised/Fear/Frightened Expression, Three-Quarter View

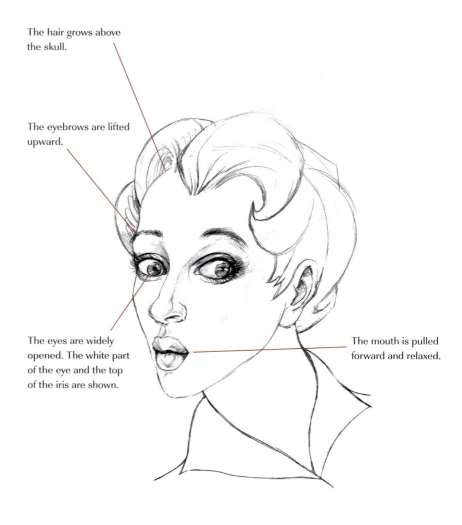

The hair grows above the skull.

The eyebrows are lifted upward.

The eyes are widely opened. The white part of the eye and the top of the iris are shown.

The mouth is pulled forward and relaxed.

2-62 Design Sample of Surprised Expression — *Crazy for You*

2-63 **Design Sample of a Surprised Expression—*Little Shop of Horrors***

ACT ONE

CRYSTAL, RONNETTE, CHIFFON

ACT TWO

LITTLE SHOP OF HORRORS
U.C.F. THEATRE SUMMER—1999

C.D. - 960
COSTUME DESIGNER
SIGNATURE

POSITIONING THE HEAD AND NECK AND DIRECTING THE EYESIGHT

Positioning the head and neck and directing eyesight are essential in establishing the mood and action of the figure in any character drawing. Striking head positions that have meaning are beneficial to the action figure, for reasons of expression and composition. A centered or tilted head, sagging or erect neck, or the direction the eyes are staring in, bring spirit and energy to the figure. An overlapping head and shoulder, squashed or stretched neck, and the various directions and angles of the face, eyesight, chest, and pelvis are all factors that play a significant role in portraying action statements.

Very little stretch and twist action produces a soft voice, whereas a big stretch and twist action produces a screaming voice. For example, front poses show a stable and motionless action. Pointing eyesight in different directions will add motion. The same applies if you draw the head at an angle to the chest and pelvis. If eyesight looks in a nonforward direction, the figure will seem more alive and expressive.

In Figure 2-64, four abstract figures show the different actions and motions in four stages/degrees. Figure 1 stands with the head, face, eyes, chest, and pelvis all facing forward, possessing little or no motion. Figure 2 stands with the chest and pelvis facing in one direction with the head in another direction while the eyes are looking off. This figure gains some motion. Figure 3 stands with the head and pelvis in one direction while the eyesight and chest are facing an opposite direction, and the head, chest, and pelvis are angled differently. The Figure 3 position presents a more interesting pose and expresses even more motion. Body movement and attitude are increased. In Figure 4, the angle degrees between the three masses and the eyesight are exaggerated some (eyes look to one side and three masses face the other side). Figure 4 shows exciting movement and attitude. Active eye motions, a stretched neck, the overlapping head and shoulder, and the swinging pelvis all convey powerful energy.

2-64 Head, Neck, and Eyesight in Relation to the Directions of the Chest and Pelvis

The active eyesight, stretched neck, overlapping head and shoulder, and pelvis swinging out all present powerful energy for the figure.

1
Eyesight, chest, and pelvis face the same directions. This displays no motion or action.

2
The head is turned in a different direction than the body, which shows little motion.

3
Figure has more movement because of the direction of the eyesight and because interesting angles are created between each mass.

4
Figure shows extreme and exciting movement and attitude because of the exaggerated angles between each mass.

3

Figure and Facial Variations

CHARACTERISTICS OF DIFFERENT AGE GROUPS

Characters in plays are a mixture of different figure types of young, old, thin, heavy, short, and tall. Knowing how to portray these characteristics and differences will help a designer portray each individual character effectively. A designer must know how to create practical costumes that will fit the criteria and attributes of a particular character.

The elements and principles of design are the fundamental foundation and key for creating and developing character figure drawings. Use various line qualities to demonstrate smooth and soft, or rough and structured silhouettes; use balance to control negative and positive space and body gestures and proportions; use contrast to accentuate fabric textures and body types; use rhythm to create body movements with draping garments; use color schemes to support and enhance your design concept; use emphasis to find the focal point of your interpretation; and use unity and harmony on the overall design ideas to keep them focused and consistent as a whole.

When drawing a child's figure, no adult proportions of the body should be considered. When drawing a child and an adult next to each other, it is easier to show the child because you can make the figure shorter. But if you are doing a play with only children, you will have no adult figure for comparison, so all the characters in the play need to be proportioned to a child's body. Whether you do a play with all children or with only some, the children need to be measured and drawn correctly to achieve an accurate and skillful design.

The drawings in Figures 3-1 through 3-6 show differences of the body types in the figures' facial expressions, actions, and gestures. Notice how the body changes at each stage of life while holding a ball. The purpose here is to show that just creating a short figure as a child or a wrinkly face as a senior is not enough. Body attitudes and actions are important elements that cannot be neglected.

Figures of differing ages are drawn with equal heights to emphasize proportions and each age group's common actions. Through this exercise, you will understand more about body proportions and attitudes, and you will be able to draw both children and adults, and thin and heavy bodies, precisely.

Chapter 1 discussed body proportions; this chapter explains more about the proportions of the body according to each body type.

3-1   Toddler

3-2   Four to Six Years

3-3   Seven to Twelve Years

3-4   Design Sample of Children's Bodies—*Tom Sawyer*

Tom Sawyer

TOM SAWYER
CWU Theatre Department

3-5 **Design Sample of Children's Bodies—*Dracula***

Girl (Beggar)

Young Lucy

Newsboy

DRACULA
Central Washington University
Theatre Arts Department

3-6   Design Sample of Children's Bodies—*Big River*

BIG RIVER
UCF THEATRE
Spring 1999

Children's Faces and Body Types

Generally speaking, children's heads are usually bigger in proportion to their bodies. A toddler's figure is about four heads tall. It is identified by a big head, small neck, chubby body, short legs, and curved body-contour lines. A four- to six-year-old body is five heads tall, with a big head, small neck, chubby body, and longer legs. A seven- to twelve-year-old body is seven heads tall and slimmer.

Children's foreheads seem bigger than adults' foreheads. Whereas the eye position of adults is located at the halfway point of their head's length, the children's eye position is below the halfway point. Children's eyebrows sit at the halfway point. A child's iris is relatively bigger, so you see less of the white part of the eye. The eye is very clear, transparent, and crystal-like. Children's noses are short, and children have round cheeks.

Children's faces are angelic and radiant. They reveal happiness, innocence, purity, curiosity, wonder, desire, life, and hope. Children's facial features convey these naïve characteristics and give children life and spirit.

Teenagers' Faces and Body Types

Teenagers are between the ages of 13 and 17. The proportions of their bodies are almost fully developed. They are eight heads tall but slimmer than adults. A teenage boy has less muscle mass than an adult male. Teenagers' bodies display youth, individuality, suppleness, boldness, insecurity, intelligence, beauty, superficial minds, experimentation, health, and innocence.

When drawing a teenager's body, keep a sense of looseness and freedom, and let the adolescent spontaneity seep through the actions. Teenagers' bodies and limbs should be relaxed and active, and their body language should show overconfident attitudes. Refer to Figures 3-7 through 3-11.

3-7   **Teenager's Body**

3-8   Design Sample of Teenager's Body—*Fame*

FAME
Department of Theatre
U.C.F.   Fall 2002

3-9   **Design Sample of Teenager's Body—***Fame*

Iris
Act I, II, & III

WRAPPED SWEATER

FAME
Department of Theatre
U.C.F.   Fall 2002

3-10 Design Sample of Teenager's Body—*Brighton Beach*

3-11 Design Sample of Teenager's Body—*Brighton Beach*

Youths' Faces and Body Types

Youth starts at 18 and progresses into the late 30s. The body is now fully developed, and this age group is at the pinnacle of life. Drawings of this age group must unveil energy, hope, high spirits, pursuits, education, desire, beauty, love, health, glamour, elegance, charm, strength, and experimentation. This group cares most about physical appearance.

Drawing bodies of youths is relatively easy because their bodies have almost no imperfections (see Figures 3-12 through 3-19). All bodies are different, but there is a basic appearance for bodies in this group, as in any other group. Female bodies have beautiful curves with an arching back, a small or wide waist, full and large breasts, and a smooth body and face. Male bodies possess beautiful and prominent bone structure, angular features, and muscles. They are handsome, strong, and healthy. When you draw the figures, keep in mind that the female body has smoother curves and the shoulder line is narrower than the hipline. The male body has angular shapes, and the shoulder line is broader than the hipline. Bodies in this age group are upright with weight over the feet and no slumping at the spine. Before you begin drawing, you should be aware of these elements.

3-12 Female Youth Face and Body

3-13 **Male Youth Face and Body**

3-14 **Design Sample of Youth's Body—*5th of July***

5TH OF JULY
UCF THEATRE 5/2003

KEN
ACT I

KEN
ACT II

C.D. - 960
COSTUME DESIGNER
SIGNATURE

3-15 Design Sample of Youth's Body—*5th of July*

3-16 Design Sample of Youth's Body—*5th of July*

3-17 Design Sample of Youth's Body—*5th of July*

3-18 Design Sample of Youth's Body—*5th of July*

3-19 Design Sample of Youth's Body — *5th of July*

5TH OF JULY
U C F THEATRE
SPRING 2003

GWEN
ACT II

C.D. - 960
COSTUME DESIGNER
SIGNATURE

Middle-Aged Faces and Body Types

When people become middle aged, they tend to lose elasticity in their skin, their beautiful, defined curves, and their healthy plumpness. Middle-aged people gain success in their careers along with gaining weight at their waistlines, bellies, and everywhere else. Under-eye bags and lines are apparent on their faces, and their legs and arms become heavy and sag. Some middle-aged people also begin to show a sagging back and silver hair.

In middle-aged bodies, illustrate overweight flabbiness and sagging flesh. The bone structures of middle-aged bodies may be the same as in youth, but the flesh has changed shape and consistency, much of it due to sun exposure. The muscles of middle-aged people diminish in firmness, smoothness, and angularity. They may possess a double chin, and their skin color becomes dull and sometimes age-spotted. See Figures 3-20 through 3-24.

3-20 Middle-Aged Female Face and Body

3-21 Middle-Aged Male Face and Body

3-22   Design Sample of Middle-Aged Body—*Big River*

BIG RIVER
UCF THEATRE
SPRING 1999

3-23 **Design Sample of Middle-Aged Body** — *5th of July*

3-24 **Design Sample of Middle-Aged Body** — *5th of July*

5TH OF JULY
UCF THEATRE
SPRING 2003

SALLY
ACT I

SALLY
ACT II

5TH OF JULY
UCF THEATRE
SPRING 2003

JUNE
ACT I

JUNE
ACT II

C.D. - 960
COSTUME DESIGNER
SIGNATURE

C.D. - 960
COSTUME DESIGNER
SIGNATURE

Elderly Faces and Body Types

When old age arrives, one's bone structure changes. The spine is no longer lean, strong, and straight, as in youth. The muscles of the body weaken and droop. A humped back and prominent belly are characteristics of senior's bodies. If the teenager is like the beginning of a blooming rose, then the senior is the withering rose. It is simply the force of nature that we all experience in our later years.

We emphasize the smoothness, radiance, strength, and durability of youthful bodies; the focus for bodies of old age is on the skin's dullness and dryness, age spots, creases, wrinkles, folds, drooping skin, hanging flesh, and a forwardly bent spine, just to name a few. To reveal these characteristics well, use proper lines, highlights, and shadows.

Older bodies can be thin or heavy. A thinner body reveals more of the protruding bone structure and develops more deep creases and wrinkle lines on the surface of the skin. A heavier body will usually form more folds and bags with puffed skin rather than deep wrinkles. See Figures 3-25 through 3-28.

3-25 **Elderly Face and Body**

3-26 Design Sample of Elderly Face and Body—*Elves and the Shoemaker*

3-27 Design Sample of Elderly Face and Body—*The Frog and Prince*

3-28   Design Sample of Elderly Face and Body—*Cinderella*

Fairy Godmother

CINDERELLA
Central Washington University
Theatre Arts Department

CHARACTERISTICS OF DIFFERENT FIGURE TYPES

Heavy Body Types

Styles of beauty change throughout time and culture. Today's ideal of beauty is a slim and slender figure, so weight problems are a constant concern. But traditional Chinese fine arts, figures in frescoes, sculptures, paintings, and pottery present humans as full and round. Almost every figure has a double chin, big ears, and a plump body. A full and round body is associated with happiness, health, wealth, grace, nobility, power, and beauty. It has been the standard of beauty and attractiveness for thousands of years. Even today, the brilliance and power of Chinese fine artwork is being shown. What was considered the ideal woman in classic Roman times would be considered very heavy by today's standards.

Large, heavy bodies carry more fat tissue than thin, bony bodies (see Figures 3-29 through 3-31). Fat tissue wraps thicker around the skeletal structures than on bony bodies. When drawing a heavy body, start with basic body proportions like we discussed in Chapter 1. Use curved body contour lines and fat tissue. If sags and bags show, such as a double chin or big belly, use fat and soft tissue rather than sculpted muscles. Emphasizing softness and roundness is the key, and stretching the tightness of the clothing will help to produce a suitable image.

3-29 Abstract Bone Structure and Body Contour Lines of Large, Heavy Bodies

3-30 Large and Heavy Body Types

Use curved contour lines to emphasize the roundness.

Large or heavy bodies have the same bone structure as thin and bony bodies have, but the fat tissue wraps thicker around the skeletal structures.

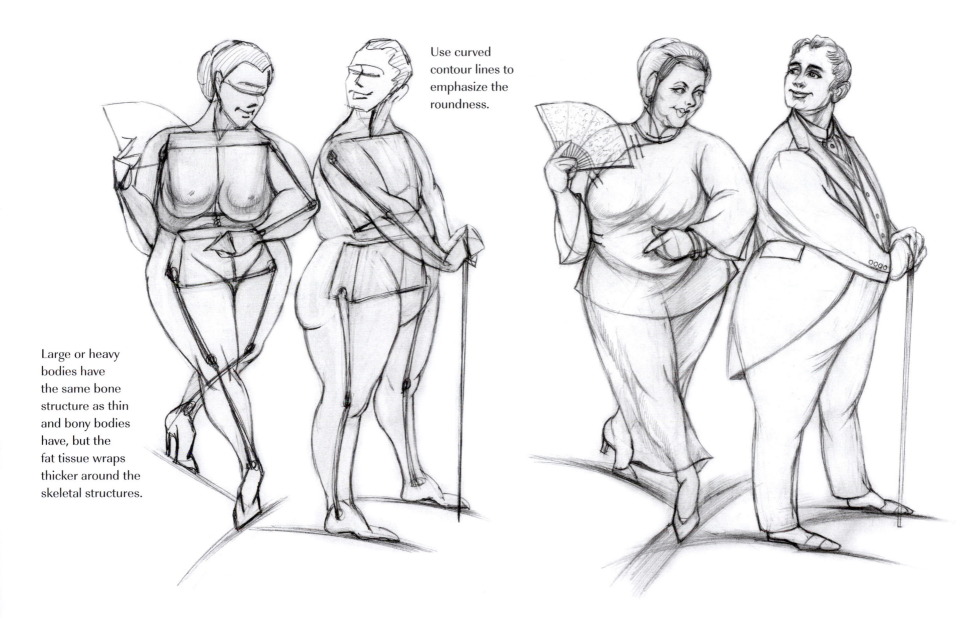

3-31 Design Sample of Large and Heavy Body—*Crazy for You*

Mother Act I

Mother Act II

Mother Act II

CRAZY FOR YOU
UCF THEATRE DEPARTMENT
SPRING 2001

Thin, Tall, or Short Body Types

A thinner body usually looks taller, and the head seems smaller; whereas the head of a short body looks larger, and the body may seem chubbier or bulkier. In China, nicknames such as *electric pole, eel, ribs,* or *stick* refer to a thin, tall body. When I create a thin body, I often think of these metaphors to inspire my imagination. Using design principles as my guide is a discipline in developing spirited character drawings and establishing effective figure poses and actions. Contrasting the body types, the thin body is very bony and crisp, and angular lines are proper for drawing the figure; curved lines are often used for female and heavy figures. The short body can be heavy or thin. It is incorrect to draw a big or small, thin or thick, narrow or wide figure without employing the principles of scale and proportion. Scale refers to the size of one object in relation to another. The principles of contrast and scale will help you start the figure.

Basic proportions of the body can apply either to thin or heavy figures (see Figures 3-32 through 3-34). However, when drawing a thin, tall body, you may cheat a little by giving a little stretch to the bone structure to emphasize the narrow, long appearance. When drawing a short body, you can shrink the bone structure a little to emphasize the short, small look. This up- or down-scale method is utilized purposely for developing character drawings.

The head of a thin, tall body generally is smaller than the head for a short, chubby body. In this case, the eight-heads-tall proportion technique may not fit in these specific figures. The thin, tall figure can be eight-and-a-half heads, and the short figure can be five to seven heads tall.

To produce an accurately proportioned body, simply keep the crotch as the dividing line that splits the upper and lower bodies in half. Then, according to the length of the torso, determine the length of the arms and the location of the bust, waistline, and pelvis line. This principle can be used for any adult body type. Keep in mind that a larger head causes the body to look shorter, and a smaller head gives the body a taller illusion.

3-32 Thin, Tall Body and Short, Chubby Body

Shrink the bone structure a little for a short body to emphasize the "short and small" look.

Keep the crotch as the dividing line that splits the upper and lower bodies in half. Then stretch the bone structure a little toward both up and down directions to emphasize the "narrow and long" appearance.

3-33 Design Sample of Tall and Thin Body—*Orphans*

3-34 **Design Sample of Tall and Thin Body**—*Amadeus*

4
Hands, Feet, and Accessories

Incorporating necessary accessories such as hats, gloves, eyeglasses, jewelry, scarves, shoes, handbags, parasols, and so forth into costume-design figures is essential for completion of the design and displaying fashions of the time. Adding necessary props such as pipes, brooms, baskets, cooking accessories, instruments, and lanterns strengthens the activity and attitude of the character and can help to represent status, personality, and mannerisms. The props added with the character tell a story. The pose designed for handling the prop brings more excitement than just a standing figure without any props displaying the costume. Therefore, incorporating accessories or props into designs shows current fashion styles, completes the design, and creates a more dramatic and expressive demeanor for the character.

HEADS AND HATS

Hats are associated with fashion and the wearer's social attitudes and status. Hats are also worn as fashionable adornments rather than just for warmth. How they are worn is a style of the time. There are three basic ways to wear hats: commonly fitted on the head, slanted at an angle, and high on top of the head. In Chapter 2, I discussed the proportions of the head and face in relation to the body. Now I will talk about adding hats in positions on the head. A hat has two basic parts: crown and brim. A common-fitted hat's crown attaches to the head's circumference; the tilted, angle-fitted hat attaches and conforms to the contour of the head; the hat sitting on top of the head attaches to the contour of the top of the head (mostly the hat sits on top of a hairdo). The following are suggestions for creating hats (see Figures 4-1 through 4-4):

🖎 Complete the shape of the head and be ready to add a hat on the head.

🖎 Establish a contact line around the head.

🖎 Build the shape of the hat—such as a crown, both crown and brim, turban, or other decorations or styles.

Completing the shape and position of the head is the foundation for creating and building the hat, because the head position affects the view of the hat. Some people do it the other way around. I suggest that you do the head first; I personally find it easier. Establishing a contact line around the head is the next step for drawing a hat. The contact line determines the look of the hat and how the hat sits on the head. The contact line for a common-fitted hat follows the circumference line of the head. The contact line for tilt-fitted hats follows the line you designed.

It can be placed more forward, backward, or tilted to one side. Once you establish the contact line, the hat continues to be drawn from that. If the hat tilts forward, consider how much of the face needs to be covered. If the hat tilts backward or sideways, consider how the hat will stay on the head.

Figures 4-5 through 4-12 are design samples of headdresses.

4-1   Female Heads and Hats in Common Positions

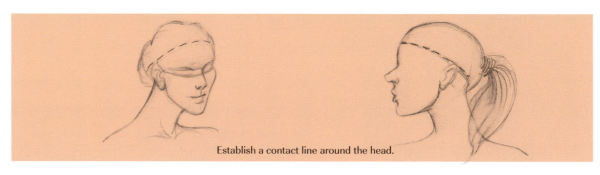

Establish a contact line around the head.

Then build the crown and add a brim to the hat.

4-2 Female Heads and Hats at Angles

4-3 Male Heads and Hats in Common Positions

Establish a contact line around the head first.

The contact line determines how a hat sits on the head.

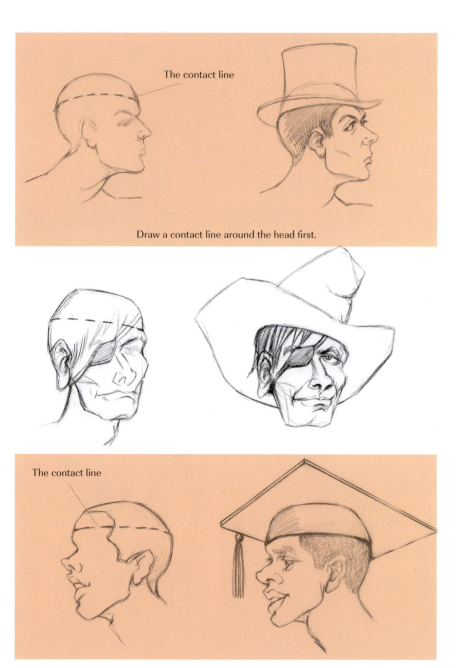

The contact line

Draw a contact line around the head first.

The contact line

4-4   **A Group of Hats**

4-5 **Design Sample of Headdress —** *The Importance of Being Earnest*

4-6 **Design Sample of Headdress—*The Importance of Being Earnest***

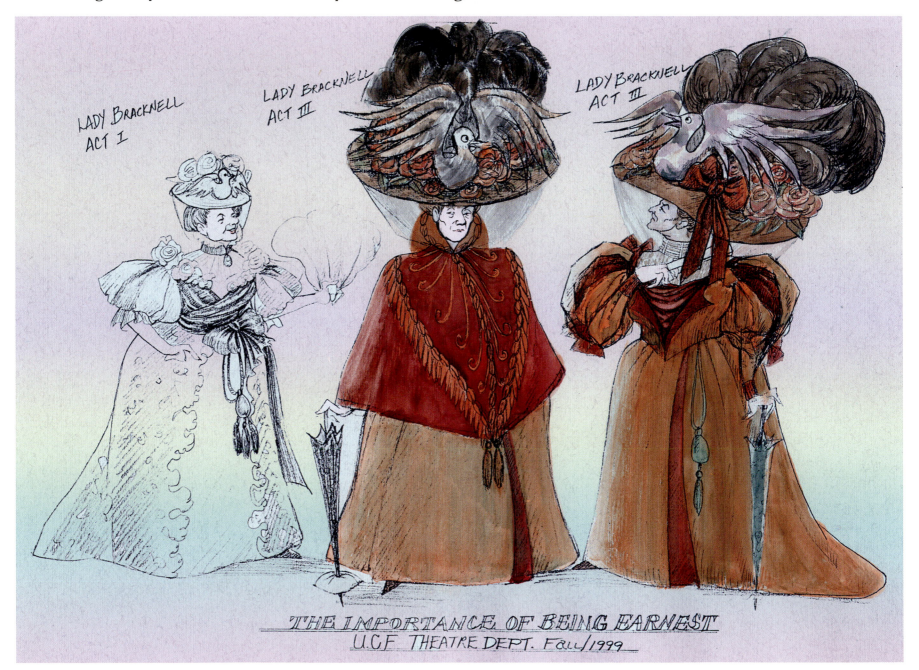

4-7   Design Sample of Headdress—*Big River*

4-8   **Design Sample of Headdress**—*Robin Hood*

ROBIN HOOD   LITTLE JOHN   WILL SCARLET   ALLEN O'DALE   STRANGER

ROBIN HOOD
CWU THEATRE ARTS DEPARTMENT

4-9   **Design Sample of Headdress—*Robin Hood***

MOTHER MEG   ROBIN HOOD   MAID MARION   FRIAR TUCK

ROBIN HOOD

CWU THEATRE ARTS DEPARTMENT

4-10 Design Sample of Headdress — *Robin Hood*

LADY MERLE   SHERIFF OF NOTINGHAM   SHERIFF'S WIFE   OLD WIDOW

ROBIN HOOD

CWU THEATRE ARTS DEPARTMENT

4-11 **Design Sample of Headdress—*Robin Hood***

King Richard

Casper

FIG. 13.
Soldier, 1450 and later, wearing hacqueton, chain hauberk, quilted gambeson. He is firing a cross-bow or arbalest.

FIG. 10.
Armor of early 14th century from a brass dated 1325. captain

ROBIN HOOD
CWU THEATRE ARTS DEPARTMENT

4-12   Design Sample of Headdress — *The Taming of the Shrew*

Petruchio

THE TAMING OF THE SHREW
Department of Theatre Arts
Utah State University

HANDS, GLOVES, AND PROPS

The hand is complex in shape and therefore difficult to draw. Sometimes I hide a hand or hands in the pockets, behind the back, or I cover the hand with a scarf or coat, for example. It is understandable to become frustrated when sketching hands, but you cannot hide hands forever. Once the character's hands are seen, we should allow them to tell a story and magnify and support the character's personality. As I mentioned, the hand is very complex, but it is not necessary to draw every detail. We are not capable of acting like a camera and catching every realistic detail. The complex details of hands can be simplified and reduced to a few basic lines and shapes. Sometimes the hands may just be a frame to suggest the action. Because of time restrictions during production periods, we all work under pressure and don't have much time to do everything in detail. Abstract hands work for costume designs, but they should be well proportioned and active.

Adding accessories or props to hands portrays the personality of the character. They become part of my costume design, and accent the body's expression for a more dramatic and characteristic appearance. Accessories and props can be put on the body or held in the hands of the figure. Choosing an accessory or prop is based on the dialogue, actions, and characteristics of a particular role in a play. Pick the prop that interprets the character's status and personality. This makes the design more interesting and engaging, adds flavor and definition, and makes a clear statement about the character.

When drawing a gloved hand, the angular shapes of the knuckles diminish and look fatter than a bare hand. Wrinkles form on the glove when the finger knuckles and wrist areas bend or move. If long gloves are worn, wrinkles will form around the bent elbow area as well.

There are three things to consider before drawing a hand:

1. Note the proportions of the hand in relation to the body.

2. Pay attention to the knuckles to notice how the hand is formed.

3. Capture the angle between the hand and wrist.

Correct proportioning of the hand facilitates proper hand size. If the knuckles line up correctly, they create a logical, graceful look to the hand. Inscribing an angle between the hand and wrist enhances the gesture action of the hand.

Hand Proportions

Hand size can be measured in relation to a person's face, since the hands and face are the most exposed parts of the body. For that reason using the face as a measurement is more proper than using other body parts. The length of the hand, which runs from the tip of the middle finger to the bottom of the palm (at the wrist), approximately equals the distance from the bottom of the chin to the middle of the forehead. Naturally, of course, some people have smaller or bigger hands than this calculation.

The hand can be divided into two major sections: the palm mass and the finger mass, which are separated at the base of the fingers (see Figure 4-13). The middle finger is the longest finger. The length of the thumb is closest to the length of the pinkie finger. The first knuckle of the thumb is located at the midpoint of the palm mass.

There are two knuckles on the thumb, three on all fingers, and a wrist knob on the outer side of the wrist. The distances between the knuckles are not equal. From the bottom to the tip of each finger, the

4-13 Proportions of the Hand

The hand can be divided into two major sections: the palm mass and the finger mass.

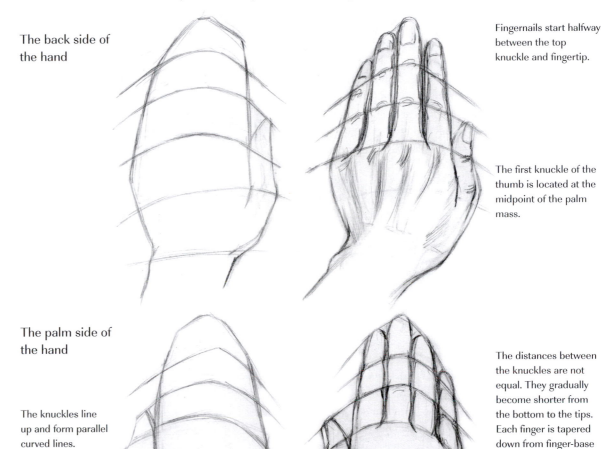

The back side of the hand

Fingernails start halfway between the top knuckle and fingertip.

The first knuckle of the thumb is located at the midpoint of the palm mass.

The palm side of the hand

The knuckles line up and form parallel curved lines.

The distances between the knuckles are not equal. They gradually become shorter from the bottom to the tips. Each finger is tapered down from finger-base to tip.

The length of the hand approximately equals the distance from the bottom of the chin to the middle of the forehead.

distance between the knuckles gradually becomes shorter. Each finger is tapered down from finger base to tip. Knuckles are bigger and more angular than the middle parts of fingers. Male knuckles are more massive and angular compared to female ones. Fingernails start halfway between the top knuckle and fingertip. Knuckles do not line up in a horizontal line but form parallel curved lines. Line up the knuckles before drawing individual fingers. Think of the form first, then fill in individual fingers. First define the bone structure of the hand rather than the soft flesh. The living hand has flesh, blood, and bone. Avoid hands that are too small.

Relationship Angle between Hand and Wrist

Most of the joints in the body can bend, twist, and rotate in different directions, within their limitations. The joint between the hand and wrist is one of them. It is capable of side-to-side and up-and-down movement. When movements take place, angles between the wrist and hand naturally occur. When drawing hands, bear in mind that hands are not isolated but are connected to the wrist, and each movement affects the wrist's movement. Thus, hands and wrists work as a unit. The proper angle creates graceful and powerful hand movements and poses. Focus attention to emphasizing the hand-to-wrist angle because achieving the precise action will effectively and favorably portray emotions. (See Figures 4-14 through 4-19.)

Figures 4-20 through 4-23 show design samples of hands and props.

4-14   Hand-Drawing Steps

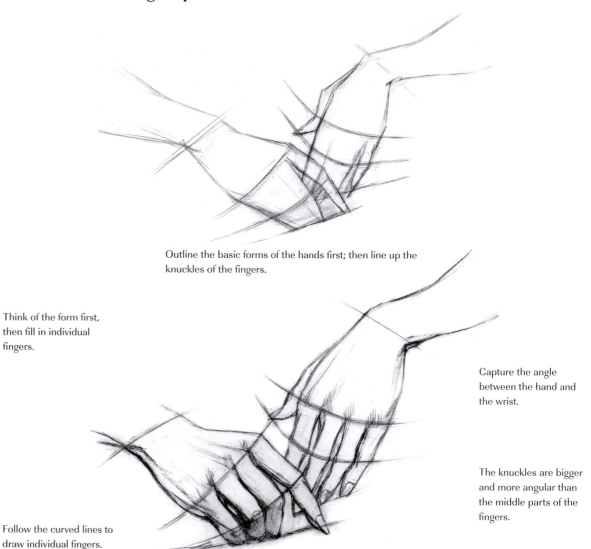

Outline the basic forms of the hands first; then line up the knuckles of the fingers.

Think of the form first, then fill in individual fingers.

Capture the angle between the hand and the wrist.

Follow the curved lines to draw individual fingers.

The knuckles are bigger and more angular than the middle parts of the fingers.

4-15 Female Hands in Action

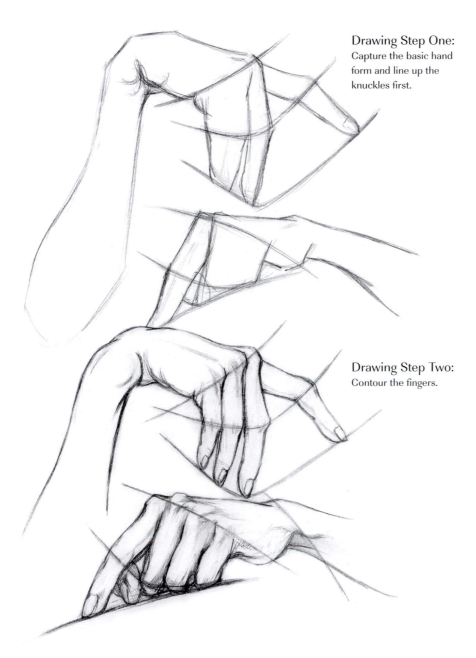

Drawing Step One: Capture the basic hand form and line up the knuckles first.

Drawing Step Two: Contour the fingers.

4-16 Variations between Angles of Hands and Wrists

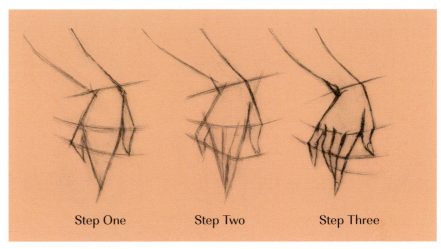

Step One   Step Two   Step Three

The proper angles between the hands and wrists create graceful and powerful hand movements and portray emotions.

4-17 Female Hands with Props

To contour the hands, follow the knuckles.

4-18 Male Hands with Props

Hands in gloves show less bone structure of the hand.

First, always outline the knuckles, then contour the fingers.

Add props that interpret the character's status and personality. This makes the design more interesting and engaging.

4-19 **Male Hands Holding Props**

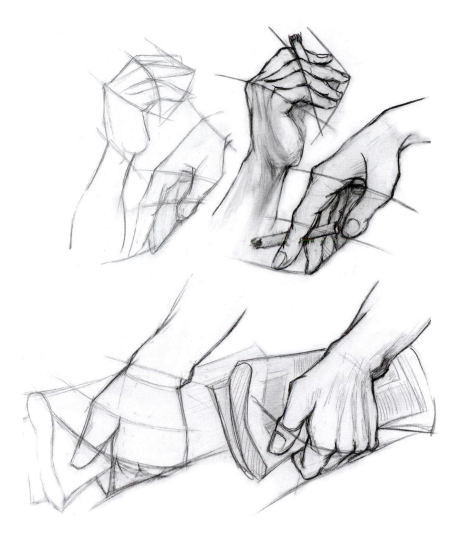

4-20   Design Sample of Hands and Props—*Dracula*

4-21 **Design Sample of Hands and Props—*Dracula***

Seamen

DRACULA
Central Washington University
Theatre Arts Department

4-22 **Design Sample of Hands and Props**—*Big River*

BIG RIVER
UCF THEATRE DEPARTMENT
SPRING 1999

4-23 Design Sample of Hands and Props—*Big River*

OVERSEER

WOMAN SLAVES

MEN SLAVES

BIG RIVER
UCF THEATRE DEPARTMENT
SPRING 1999

C.D. - 96
COSTUME DESI

SIGNATURE

FEET AND SHOES

Feet are another difficult body part to draw, but still a bit easier to draw than hands. As with hands, studying feet proportions before drawing is the most effective and efficient way to learn (see Figure 4-24). In other drawing books, they say the length of the foot equals the length of the forearm when the arm is bent, which I have found to be true. Foot size relates to a person's height. Taller people have proportionally longer arms in comparison to their feet, compared to shorter people; this ratio adjusts accordingly.

When drawing feet, keep in mind the following:

❧ The inner side of the bottom of the foot forms an arch line in order to support body weight. The top of the foot also forms an arch line parallel to the bottom inner arch.

❧ The inner side of the bottom of the foot is much thicker than the outer side of the foot.

❧ The outer side of the foot is relatively flat as it touches the ground.

❧ The heel of the foot is ball-shaped.

Ankle bones are the key in placing feet in proper position. The inner ankle bone is higher than the outer ankle bone in both females and males. Female ankle bones have smooth curves and male ankle bones are angular and big. When drawing feet as in drawing hands, the angle is very important. Capturing the correct and proper angle of the ankle bone between the legs and feet makes the feet appear strong and lifelike. When drawing high-heeled shoes, the angle between the leg and foot diminishes to some degree depending on the height of the heel (see Figure 4-25). The taller the heel, the smaller the angle.

4-24 Proportions of the Feet

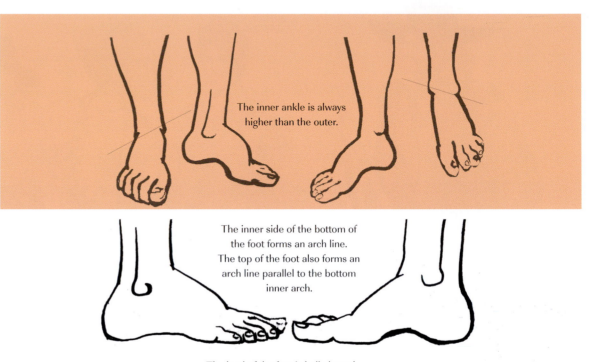

The inner ankle is always higher than the outer.

The inner side of the bottom of the foot forms an arch line. The top of the foot also forms an arch line parallel to the bottom inner arch.

The heel of the foot is ball-shaped.

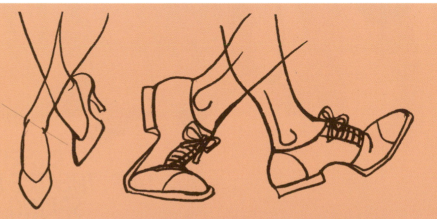

The length of the foot equals the length of the forearm when the arm is in bending position.

4-25 Female Feet and Shoes

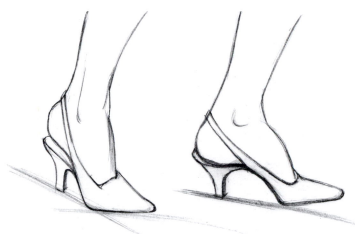

Female ankle bones have smooth curves.

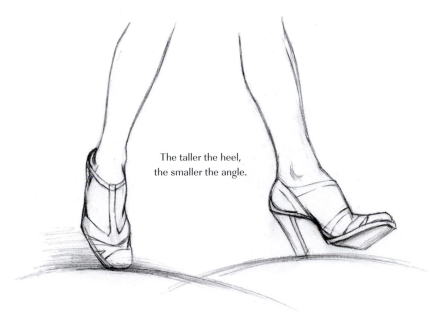

The taller the heel, the smaller the angle.

When drawing high-heeled shoes, the angle between the leg and foot diminishes to some degree, depending on the height of the heel.

When checking feet for size and shape, keep in mind:

- Use the correct length/proportion/size of the feet in relation to the body.

- There are arch lines at both the top and bottom of the foot.

- Make ball-shaped heels.

- Use correct angles at the anklebones.

- The inner ankle is always higher than the outer.

Shoes are made to fit the feet. Once you know how to draw feet, the shoes will simply be drawn over the feet. Figure 4-26 contains a few sketches showing the feet and shoes overlapping each other. You are able to see the foot beneath the shoe, and hopefully this helps you to understand how the shoe fits the foot. Be aware that the soles of shoes are like feet: inner soles of shoes have deeper curves, and outer soles of shoes are relatively straighter with shallower curves. The deep and shallow curves show which shoes are right or left. Figures 4-27 through 4-31 are design samples of feet and shoes.

4-26 **Male Feet and Shoes**

The inner anklebone is higher than the outer anklebone.

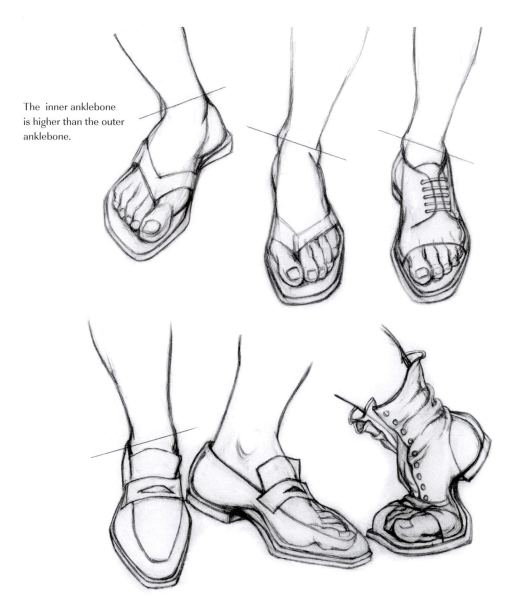

Capturing the proper angle between the legs and feet makes the feet appear strong and lifelike.

4-27 Design Sample of Feet and Shoes—*Grease*

GREASE
DANNY.

4-28   **Design Sample of Feet and Shoes — *Grease***

Kenickie

Kenickie

GREASE
Central Washington University
Theatre Arts Department

4-29   **Design Sample of Feet and Shoes—*Grease***

GREASE
Central Washington University
Theatre Arts Department

4-30 **Design Sample of Feet and Shoes—*Grease***

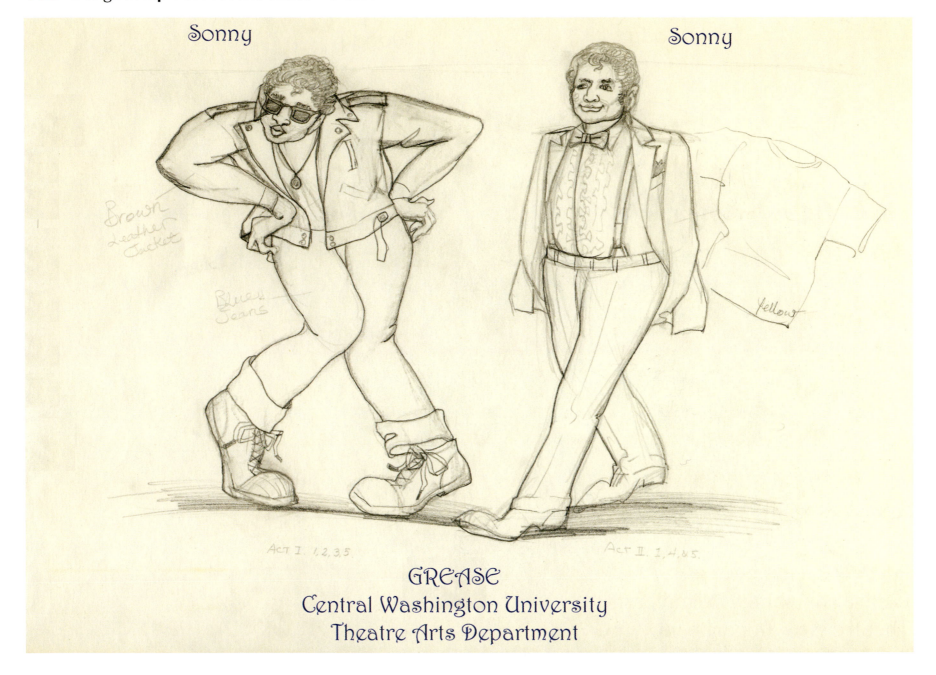

Sonny

Sonny

Brown
Leather
Jacket

Blue
Jeans

Yellow

Act I. 1, 2, 3, 5.

Act II. 1, 4, & 5.

GREASE
Central Washington University
Theatre Arts Department

4-31 Design Sample of Feet and Shoes—*Grease*

Vince Fontaine

Johnny Casino

Cha-Cha

gold trim

ACT II. 1

gold trim
ACT II

ACT II 1

GREASE
Central Washington University
Theatre Department

5
Character Costume Design Creation

As a costume designer, I want to portray my designs visually and structurally to bring my characters to life. The visual images convey information about the design concept, and the structural elements are the body's active forms and detailed garments. Both tie together and cannot be parted. Characters in a play may be humans, animals, or spirits. The costume designer portrays them as main characters, supporting characters, or ensembles. The historical accuracy of the costumes, manners of the time period, and elements of style in presentation are crucial. How to develop different types of character figures for diverse types of plays with proper poses and facial expressions is a challenge and requires conscious effort to elegantly and correctly define the character's personalities and attitudes.

In character figure drawings, the designer is confronted by three components: the body, the facial expression, and the style and the texture of the garment. A costume designer's task is to combine these three components.

All the figures in this chapter show the three steps involved in creating character figures:

Step One: Search for actions and movements.

Step Two: Search for what the figure is doing beneath the garments.

Step Three: Complete the figure with a detailed costume.

WHAT IS THE BEST WAY TO BEGIN?

Movements and attitudes of characters differ according to the type of production: drama, musical, comedy, dance, children's play, and so on. A vivid character pose presents the spirit of the character and enhances the design concept. Before composing a figure pose, conduct an analysis of the play and character first. Without fully learning everything about the character's appearance and personality and the time period, it is hard to create a proper action or movement for the figure.

Development of a character figure drawing is based on the elements and theme of the play. After reading the play and analyzing the characters, I usually choose some important actions, lines, dialogue, music, or symbolic factors from the play to blend in with my character. The composition of the pose should express and carry out the actions and attitudes of the character from that play. For example, in the development of my costume design for the two sisters in *Arsenic and Old Lace*—Abby and Martha—the play title represents a symbol. *Old lace* implies an elder, and *arsenic* is the chemical around which the conflict revolves. The plot of the play focuses on these two lovable yet destructive sisters who poison people with arsenic. In this farcical comedy play, the two old siblings bring laughter and joy to the audience through their absurd actions. The costume figure poses should support and combine the play's theme and the actions and personalities of the characters. They should show the elderly bodies and faces. I composed the two sisters pouring arsenic as the gesture for both of them to indicate their main focus and action and the play's main theme. I consider this action a dramatic moment in the play, and the theme ties in with my illustrations. The sisters' facial features exhibit cartoon expressions rather than realistic expressions to show their comical actions in killing people with indifference and secrecy and without compassion.

Abby has a round and portly body, and Martha has a thin, bony, tall body. This contrast produces more humor. The lace trims on their costumes also emphasize the title and theme of the play.

This is the basic way I develop particular figure gestures and poses for all my designs. When designing costumes for musicals or dance plays, I incorporate music and body rhythm to present the movement and flow of the body, and produce a realistic impression of how the costumes fit and work with the body. If the costume design is for an animal character and the actor's body is completely covered by the costume, I try to show the layers of the costume to indicate how the actor moves inside of the costume.

Usually after reading the script and analyzing the characters, I make a rough-draft layout to arrange the costume-sequence changes from scene to scene and to find out how many figures I must create. Secondly, I categorize the characters based on their relationships to one another and decide whether to put them on the same page, if needed. You will notice that some of my costume designs in this book are grouped either showing one character in sequence costume changes or related characters together. Advantages to grouping figures on the same page are to clearly show costume-sequence changes between scenes and acts; to provide an easy way to notice contrasts in colors, textures, and styles of the costumes; and to save paper and portfolio storage space. The disadvantages include insufficient space when noting fabric swatches on the page, and that mistakes on one figure on the page will destroy whatever drawings were previously on that paper.

As mentioned before, three-quarter and extreme three-quarter views are used more often than other views. It is a popular choice for many costume designers because this view reveals many angles of the body and displays adequate representation for the costume. It is sometimes necessary to draw the back view if it is very helpful in displaying the garment style. An appropriate pose will show the garment to its best advantage. It will enhance the design concept and help the director, actors, and construction team visualize the costume as it will appear on stage.

My suggestions for drawing character figures are the following:

- Make every line meaningful.

- Visualize the figure in a head-to-toe concept on the page as you draw.

- Focus on proportion, balance, unity, and action first. Then emphasize the facial expressions.

- Check your sketch for proportion and balance, and make sure your character's movement looks comfortable by looking at it from the reverse side of the paper, through a mirror, or holding the paper upside down. These checking methods will help you see awkward lines and shapes that aren't as noticeable from the front of the paper. Try this, and it will surprise you.

PROPORTION, ACTION, AND MOVEMENT

If my figure does not show the movement or emotions I want, I just keep altering and redrawing it over and over again until I am satisfied. My figures must talk to me and communicate a certain vibe, one that impressively portrays the character with a *Wow!* They must speak, act, and express moods and feelings. I see my characters in action; if you see your characters that way, you will force them to make noises, move, be lifelike, and have attitudes and personalities.

Drawing from head to toe is the principle for all figure drawings. Consider the basic bone structures at the beginning stages. Capture body movement and action, and correctly locate the weight-supporting foot/feet before developing facial expressions and hand gestures. Body movement should collaborate with perfect facial and hand expression as a whole to communicate a beautiful, suitable pose. Make sure all relationships between body parts work and support each other before continuing with details of the three major masses of the body (head, chest, and pelvis), the head and facial features, the head and neck, the head and shoulders, and chest and pelvis with the limbs. Before drawing any features on the head, make sure the angle between the head, neck, and shoulders is properly showing the action and telling a story. Before starting the arms, make sure the angle between the chest and pelvis shows movement. Most of the time, the arms are drawn before the hands; however, an outlined hand frame can be drawn before the arm (especially bending arms). Then adjust the position of the arm and add individual fingers.

When creating movements or actions, define the action line or the body centerline. The body centerline runs from the pit of the neck to the crotch and down to the weight-supporting foot or feet. Correctly locating the weight-supporting foot or feet is the key to balancing the body (more details are mentioned in Chapter 1). Remember, the centerline is straight when the body is in an erect position and curved when the body is in action. The body centerline/action line shows the flow of the movement and the action.

Joints control all movements (see Chapter 1 for more details). Knowing the locations of the joints, how they work, and their limitations are ways to improve how you draw a figure in motion. Each joint is like a break-point for each part of the body. Use and manipulate these break-points to measure and adjust the proportions of the body and to compose body movements.

Using abstract bone structure is the easiest way to start a design figure, especially when drawing from imagination. Keeping the figure well-balanced, well-proportioned, and well-structured with motions is enough to focus on at once during the beginning stages of a drawing. Simplified, abstract bone-structure lines and shapes help to establish proportion and movement at the beginning stage.

Use basic action lines to portray the attitude and movements of the character. This is the foundation for all figure drawings, since costume designers usually start sketches without any human models. The greatest benefit of abstract gestures is that they eliminate a lot of meandering lines and shapes that are messy and meaningless to the character.

Using simple lines and shapes is an essential and fast way to begin with easy control. With the stick figure, all the joints are exposed, so it is easier to manipulate body parts to achieve the desired pose or gesture. Creating a figure pose is like building a house or bridge—the foundation has to be solid. The stick figure will be the foundation and the frame of the body. Without a good foundation, you cannot continue building without failing.

In your design, consider the height of the figure, the direction it is facing, what the arms are doing, where the feet are located, how the feet are positioned, and the bending or twisting angles between the head and shoulders, the chest, pelvis, arms, and legs. These factors should be compared, contrasted, and combined while drawing to achieve the perfect pose most suitable for the character. The easiest way to begin is to establish correct proportions and preferred action. Keep the figure drawing head-to-toe principle in mind as you draw. Do not detail every spot on the figure before outlining the basic shape.

The first five steps in figure drawing follow. It is critical to perform these five steps at the beginning of figure drawing. This helps to quickly establish and prepare a solid and accurate foundation of proportion and movement and avoids getting into details too early.

1. Start with two marks at the top and bottom of the paper to determine how tall the figure is going to be.

2. Quickly draw a middle mark in the center of the two marks to indicate the crotch line. This is the first step in controlling the proportions of the body (see Chapter 1 for more on proportion).

3. Indicate the body centerline/action line with either a straight or curved line, according to the pose. An erect body possesses a straight action line, and a body in action possesses a curved one. Defining the action line captures the action and motion of the figure. The action line is considered a head-to-toe concept, establishing the sense of movement of the body.

4. Outline the head mass and add two lines to indicate the shoulder and hip. These two lines cross the straight or curved body centerline. These two lines may be tilted or angled, depending on whether the movement is mild or extreme.

5. Locate the weight-supporting leg/legs and foot/feet. The weight-supporting legs and foot/feet should be placed where the center of gravity line ends, for solid stabilization of the body. The center of gravity line starts from the pit of the neck and goes directly down to the ground (see Chapter 1 for more on the center of gravity line).

After you complete all five steps, draw the rest of the body parts. Outline the chest and pelvis. Remember that the head, chest, and pelvis are joined by the spine, move independently of each other, and move in opposite directions for balance. Don't forget the units: head and facial features, chest and arms, and pelvis and legs. Each unit works and moves as a whole. All the sketching outlines for establishing the figure pose should be light lines, and shapes should be used as guidelines. Now you are ready for the next step, contouring the body.

WHAT IS THE FIGURE DOING BENEATH THE GARMENTS?

Contouring a figure means following the basic skeleton frame (abstract or stick-bone structures are used as the basic skeleton frame in this book). All body movements are governed by the structure of the skeleton. A good foundation skeleton frames the shape of the surface and silhouette of the body. Contouring the figure is defining muscle curves and forms of the body. The characteristics of body type and move-

ment affect how garments rest on the body. Step one in this chapter is the foundation for contouring the body. Natural curves and shapes of body muscles are what contour the figure. This creates a manner of roundness to the figure and automatically produces guidelines for drawing garments.

Comparison of the lines, shapes, and proportions of body parts is the key for contouring. (Blocking in figures and contouring curved lines and shapes of the body were discussed in Chapter 1, and differences in body types was discussed in Chapter 3). Comparing body-part proportions helps to contour and distinguish curves and shapes of the body. For example, some body-contour lines overlap, one in front of the other, when curved muscles form. Both outlines of the shoulder and forearm muscle overlap the biceps outline. Both contouring lines of the thighs and lower legs overlap the knee lines. The outer lines of the neck overlap the shoulder-slope lines. The cheekbone line overlaps the jawlines. By now you should notice that the outlines of the prominent or greater parts of the body stay forward, and the nonprominent parts stay behind.

Contouring a figure runs from head to feet with the head-to-toe concept:

1. When contouring the head, proportion it to the height of the body and set it at an angle with the shoulder line to create action and motion.

2. When contouring facial features, line them up along the centerline of the face.

3. The collarbone and the pit of the neck should always be well-defined in both males and females.

4. When contouring shoulders, compare them to the hipline to capture the angles between the chest and pelvis, the direction the body is facing, and the hip-swinging motions.

5. When contouring the upper arm, define the overlapping shapes of the arm.

6. When contouring the female bust, cleavage is emphasized and contour lines should be smooth and fine. A man's chest is muscular and contoured with angular lines.

7. When contouring legs, notice that the inner contour line is relatively straighter than the outer contour line, due to the curve of the thigh. Be aware of the level differences of curves on the lower leg. The point at which the outer calf is at its fullest curve is higher and slightly bigger than the fullest point on the inner curve.

8. When contouring anklebones, keep the inner anklebone higher than the outer one.

9. When contouring hands, compare them with the size of the face because in most cases, both the hands and the face are exposed. Create an angle between the hand and wrist to add some motion and life to the hand.

10. When contouring feet, check their proportions with the forearm. Create an angle between the feet for gracefulness and stability. Double check the location of the feet with the center of gravity line. Make sure the weight-supporting legs and foot/feet are placed where the center of gravity line ends, for stability.

Overall, use continuous contour lines for female bodies to show smooth body curves. Broken contour lines are often used on male bodies to emphasize a muscular silhouette. A heavier body possesses thicker fat tissue around the bone structure. Thin bodies have thin muscle tissue. Tall figures have smaller heads, and short figures may have relatively bigger heads and shorter arms and legs. Remember that bones do not stretch, but the muscles can be stretched. Only joints can bend, and bending joints show joint knobs. The muscles around joint areas form creases or wrinkled lines.

Most of the time, costume designers must create figures from their imagination. Having a live model may not be practical due to the typically tight budgets in theatre. This situation demands that designers be clever and inventive. Concentrate mainly on primary principal muscles for body parts. Keep in mind that the shape of each body part is a three-dimensional form. The human body is an extremely complex entity with structures, movements, and functions that are related and interconnected. Creating realistically styled figure drawings is the aim and goal for designing costumes. However, using an expanding cartoon concept—extreme and simple—to develop character figures is another way of creating character drawings. The "extreme" is the exaggeration of energy, movements, and facial expressions. The "simple" is the stylized, significant, bold, flowing, and firm contour lines and shapes that define the actions and attitudes of the character. The combination of realistic and stylized impressions adds dramatic excitement and personality to the figures.

DETAILED COSTUMES

The silhouette of a garment usually automatically follows the body contour lines (except over hoop skirts) and reflects body contours. The choice of pose is essential to making costumes flattering because it displays important design elements such as style and fabrication, depicts the character's attitude, and shows how the garments move over the body.

A well-stylized and impressive figure body is the foundation for drawing garments. The garments must integrate easily with the body.

Suggestions for defining garments are:

1. Follow contour lines and shapes of the body when you contour garments, and treat the body as a cylindrical three-dimensional form.

2. Use necessary wrinkles and folds on the garments to define body joints.

3. Use the proper lines to define the texture of a garment and to capture the way a garment hangs.

To achieve those three objectives:

🌊 **Follow body contour lines and shapes to contour the garments.** The openings of a jacket include the neckline, sleeve cuffs, and the bottom of the jacket. The openings of a shirt include the neckline, short/long sleeves, and the hemline. The openings of pants are the waist and cuffs. The openings of a skirt are the waist and hem. Defining these openings on the body affects the form of the body. An easy way to envision the openings is to visualize the shape of the openings as a circle; these circles fit over a cylindrical body form. They are not horizontal lines or square shapes. The same principle should be used for drawing the waistline, yolk of the garment, and stripes. Keep in mind that the human body doesn't have flat surfaces; it is a three-dimensional cylindrical form.

🌊 **Use necessary wrinkles and folds on garments to define body joints.** A garment conforms to the structure of the body. Many wrinkles and folds appear on garments when a figure is in action. Try to catch major actions that define movements by emphasizing the wrinkles and folds associated with the movement, in relation to where the body joints bend or twist.

The folds or wrinkles of the garments reveal the locations of the joints and their associated bones (includes shoulder blades, rib cage, and pelvis) and muscle structures. Common areas where stress wrinkles and folds can be seen are at the crotch, armpit, bust, waistline, and bends of the elbows and knees. Be aware that when the garment rests or touches the body, body forms and joints are revealed. When the garment falls away from the body, the body part is hidden (see Chapter 1 for more information on garments in relation to the body in action).

🌊 **Use the proper lines to define garment textures and to capture the way a garment hangs or lays on the body.** The style of a garment is determined by its silhouette. The silhouette can be slim and boxy, clinging and rigid-fitted, or tight. Fabrics can be light or dark, crisp or soft. Garment details can be large and exaggerated, dramatic, or small and subtle. Using effective lines in drawing these elements can produce extraordinary and exciting work. The necessary costume details will help the director and construction team visualize the actual garment.

Outlining the Garment

🌊 **Collar.** The collar encircles the neck and frames the face. Pay attention to the collar because it is the focal point of the garment and shows the style of the garment. Most collars are symmetrically curved around the neck (some collars are asymmetrically cut) and balanced at both sides of the neck. A collar goes around the neck and follows the shape of the neck.

❧ **Tie.** The tie is another article of clothing that is of central focus. It is a small piece but plays a significant role in showing the personality and status of a character. It accents the design concept. When drawing the tie, show how it is tied or how it hangs if untied. Also show pattern and size—the more details, the better.

❧ **Sleeves.** Sleeves are affected by shoulder treatments. If sleeves are made of soft material, they will reveal the natural shoulder contour line in a soft silhouette. If a garment has shoulder pads, the natural shoulder widens and becomes square-shaped, and the sleeves show a tailored silhouette. Of course, a leg-of-mutton sleeve will be a larger-scaled sleeve. If the arm is bent, wrinkles and folds should be emphasized at the elbow area.

❧ **Bodices.** The bodices can be rigid, fitted, or loosely fitted. The neckline, bustline, and waistline should be defined. Use bold and strong continuous lines to draw rigid, fitted, or tailored bodices. Use soft curvy lines to draw the bust and necklines. The waistline is not a horizontal line but follows the body contour shapes.

❧ **Pockets.** Pockets are usually symmetrically sewn on both sides of a garment. They may have square or round corners, flaps or no flaps. They can be welted pockets or patched pockets, and can be topstitched or not. All these structural details affect the style of a garment. Make them clearly stated and well defined.

❧ **Pants.** When drawing a pair of dress pants, emphasize crease lines for a tailored look. When the leg bends, it creates wrinkles and folds at the knee area and reveals the shapes of the thigh and kneecap. When the leg is in a straight position, make two breaks on the crease line at the knee and ankle areas (some include the sides of the pants) to indicate joints for a more realistic look. Stress wrinkles at the crotch area occur with any type of pants. Clean and crisp lines give a tailored impression. Soft and smooth lines show the soft silhouette of pants and the smooth-textured material. Broken or short lines show a sagging, ragged look. Jeans are usually fitted to the body so show more leg form and no crease lines, and they show more wrinkles and folds than dress pants.

❧ **Skirts.** Skirts are a wide or narrow circular tube. The bottom of the hem is never drawn straight across from one side to the other. Visually, the hemline is a big circular ring hung over the cylindrical shaped body. The hemline is curved due to the perspective aspect. Some skirts may have asymmetrical hemlines. In this case, hemlines may be treated differently, but keep in mind that the body is a cylindrical form.

❧ **Pleats.** Pleats can be box or knife pleats and are normally regular in shape. Pleats often use crisp, sharp, and linear lines to give a tailored look. The gatherings usually possess a full and bulky silhouette. Draw gatherings with broken or irregular lines to show fullness and body. The hem outline of the pleated skirt will show angular, sharp corners; the hem outline of the gathered skirt will show curvy, waved lines.

❧ **Ruffles.** Ruffles can be straight or circular in cut. Straight ruffles tend to be crisper and fuller than circular ruffles, which show a soft curved silhouette. When drawing ruffles, always establish the control line first. The top control line will be the stitching line, and the other line is the bottom of the ruffles. The bottom line is curved waves and uneven or irregular. Next, draw uneven ease lines and connect them to the control line to create an illusion of fullness and shape.

The Details

Design costumes in detail, combining emphasis on the face, hairstyle, and accessories. Express the total design concept by drawing in the positions of the pockets, size of lapels and buttons, bold or subtle trims, darts, seams, inserts, specific linings, underwear, and so forth. All details should be proportioned and balanced with the garment as a whole, and the body should display rhythm, harmony, and unity. The final costume should express an overall concept of attitude and flatter the characteristics of the role.

If adding accessories completes the design as a whole, adding props to the figure can enhance the action of the character. Props or accessories are alive and take an active part in the pose. They become part of the costume design, accent the body for a more dramatic effect, and they give the character his/her intended appearance.

5-1 *Arsenic and Old Lace*

| **STEP ONE** Search for Actions and Movements | **STEP TWO** Search for What the Figure Is Doing Beneath the Garments | **STEP THREE** Complete the Figure with a Detailed Costume |

C.D. - 960
COSTUME DESIGNER

- The theory is: The most important element in a drawing is the gesture, and that has to be established before proceeding with the details.

- The twist of the body and the weight-bearing foot give a definite spirit and create drawings that entertain.

- The easy way to think about it is this: **Get the proportions right first!**

- The tendency to start at one spot on the figure in detail and proceed to finish the drawing without the proportions drawn right usually results in failure.

- Here is a quote from artist Walter Stanchfield: "We search with the pen or pencil, ferreting to modify and enhance the gesture. We're not just copying arms and legs; we are trying to capture the spirit of the gesture, to create the information you seek is not the way a camera would record. You go beyond that to an almost psychic reading of the inner motivation. Draw verbs, not nouns."

5-2 *Arsenic and Old Lace*

STEP ONE Search for Actions and Movements	STEP TWO Search for What the Figure Is Doing Beneath the Garments	STEP THREE Complete the Figure with a Detailed Costume

• **Get the proportions right first!**

• Adding props or accessories to the figure will help show the personality of the character. The props or accessories are alive and are taking an active part in the pose. They become part of the costume design. Use flowing, contrasting action lines to accent the body for a more dramatic effect, to give the "characteristic appearance."

5-3 *Arsenic and Old Lace*

STEP ONE Search for Actions and Movements

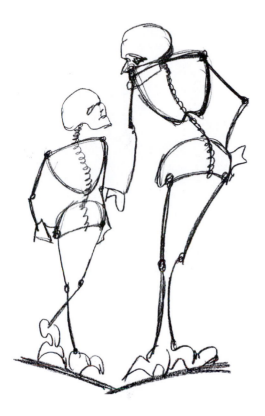

STEP TWO Search for What the Figure Is Doing Beneath the Garments

STEP THREE Complete the Figure with a Detailed Costume

- **Get the proportions right first!**

- The most important element in a drawing is the gesture, and that has to be established before proceeding with the details.

- Look for simple, basic action lines of the figure that delineate the story, attitude, or action of the character.

- Block in the figures; contour the curved lines of the body.

5-4 *Death of a Salesman*

STEP ONE Search for Actions and Movements

STEP TWO Search for What the Figure Is Doing Beneath the Garments

STEP THREE Complete the Figure with a Detailed Costume

MISS FORSYTHE
ACT II

LETTA
ACT II

C.D. - 960
TUME DESIGNER

- **Get the proportions right first!**
- Emphasis on the body language

- The body shape and the movement qualities help to define the character.
- Give the figures a characteristic appearance.
- Block in the figures; contour the curved lines of the body.

5-5 *Death of a Salesman*

STEP ONE Search for Actions and Movements	**STEP TWO** Search for What the Figure Is Doing Beneath the Garments	**STEP THREE** Complete the Figure with a Detailed Costume

• **Get the proportions right first!**

• Block in the figures; contour the curved lines of the body.

5-6 *Peter Pan*

STEP ONE Search for Actions and Movements

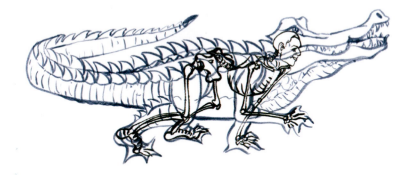

STEP THREE Complete the Figure with a Detailed Costume

STEP TWO Search for What the Figure Is Doing Beneath the Garments

- The theory is: The most important element in a drawing is the gesture, and that has to be established before proceeding with the details.

- The body shape and the movement qualities help to define the character. **Draw verbs, not nouns!**

5-7 *Peter Pan*

STEP ONE Search for Actions and Movements

STEP TWO Search for What the Figure Is Doing Beneath the Garments

STEP THREE Complete the Figure with a Detailed Costume

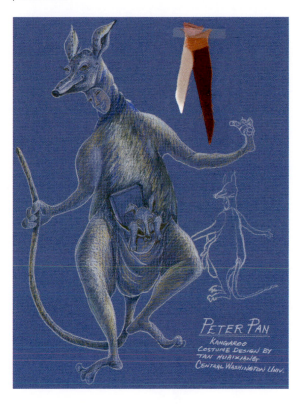

- Look for simple, basic action lines of the figure that delineate the attitude of the character.

- Block in the figures; contour the curved lines of the body.

5-8 *Peter Pan*

STEP ONE Search for Actions and Movements	STEP TWO Search for What the Figure Is Doing Beneath the Garments	STEP THREE Complete the Figure with a Detailed Costume

PETER PAN
LION
COSTUME DESIGN BY
TAN HUAIXIANG
CENTRAL WASHINGTON UNIV.

- The most important element in a drawing is the gesture, and that has to be established before proceeding with the details.

- The twist of the body and the weight-bearing foot give a definite spirit and create drawings that entertain.

- Block in the figure; contour the curved lines of the body.

5-9 *Peter Pan*

| STEP ONE Search for Actions and Movements | STEP TWO Search for What the Figure Is Doing Beneath the Garments | STEP THREE Complete the Figure with a Detailed Costume |

- The twist of the body and the weight-bearing foot give a definite spirit and create drawings that entertain.

- Contour the curved lines of the body.
- Give the figure a "characteristic appearance".

6

Rendering Techniques

CREATING HIGHLIGHTS AND SHADOWS

The purpose of putting highlights and shadows on a figure is to define and contour the features and shapes of the body, and to create garment value and texture. Properly applying highlights and shadows brings out descriptive character, enhances effectiveness of design details, and contributes to the mood of the character. Shadows and highlights can be dramatic, exaggerated, or subtle. Artists in the fine arts may use more extreme lights, shadows, and cast shadows to create dramatic and exciting compositions of subjects that express their emotional experiences and intensify the mood of the artwork. However, suggested and simple highlights and shadows are used for costume figure drawings in this book because too much shadow affects garment texture and color. Shadow less on the face than the body parts to focus on facial expressions.

Adding highlights and shadows adds value to the object. *Value* is the degree of light or dark on the surface of fabrics. Value describes shape and texture and the space in which the object is surrounded. In costume character drawing, use value to create descriptive garments and figures. When light hits an object, highlights and shadows are present. Highlights and shadows create a three-dimensional object because they indicate depth and distinguish texture.

There is a basic pattern to forming highlights, shadows, and reflected lights coming from all directions. There are two basic planes of light and dark. The side of an object facing the light is brighter in value. In the light plane, there are highlights, and in the dark plane, include a very dark boundary line and reflected light. A highlight is the brightest area that light hits directly. The boundary line is where light and dark sides meet (or where the surface of the object turns). The boundary line is darkest in value in the dark plane of an object. There is a gray tone in the dark plane, which is lighter than the boundary line but darker than reflected light. Reflected light bounces back from surrounding objects or surfaces. It is lighter in the shadow area, but not any brighter than the value of the light plane. Reflected light takes place on the outer edge of an object on the dark shadow side and is a very important element in defining three-dimensional shape and form. The cast shadow is the darkest among all shadows and has the sharpest edge. In conclusion, the six elements of creating highlights and shadows are light side, highlight, boundary line, dark side, reflected light, and cast shadow.

Hard and soft edges appear on objects due to the shape of an object. When light hits a round object, the boundary line is soft, and a gradual transition from light to dark takes place. When light hits an angular object (such as a box), it produces a hard-edged boundary line. The hard-edged boundary line is created by the sharp turn on the object. Hard edges can be seen on a human body at the nose bridge, jawline, and the outline of the lips. Soft edges show up on nonflat surfaces such as the forehead, cheekbones, arms, legs, and torso. Soft edges often occur on human bodies because of their cylindrical forms. To create a soft edge, develop a medium tone between the light side and the boundary line for a gradual transition of subtle turning.

Adding highlights and shadows transforms a two-dimensional form into a three-dimensional illusion. Here are some suggestions for shadowing a costume design figure:

- Complete the outline of the figure and garment.

- Determine the boundaries where the form turns between lights and shadows of the figure and garment.

- Organize and simplify the shadows.

- Fill the shadow areas with middle-toned hatching/cross-hatching lines.

- Further define light and dark boundaries or division lines where the form turns.

- Create soft transition edges due to the cylindrical shape of the body.

- Depict reflected light by darkening or erasing nearby shadows.

- When you're finished, look over the figure. There should be a high contrast between the light and dark sides of hard-edged shadows and a low contrast in soft-edged shadows.

A light source coming from above will define the shapes of the upper portions of features; the perimeter of the features' lower portions will be determined by shadows and reflecting lights from underneath at the bottom edges (see Figure 6-1).

Light from below is reversed from light from above: Light areas will usually be the eye sockets, the bottom of the nose, the top lip, under the lower lip, and under the chin. The bottom of the bust will have more noticeable light than other areas on garments. Boundary lines on features are usually seen along the curved bone of the eyesocket, the tip of the nose, the edge of the upper lip, the top of the cheekbones, the edge of the jawline, and the middle of the bustline (see Figure 6-2).

6-1 Light from Above

Light coming from above will define the shapes of the upper portions of the features.

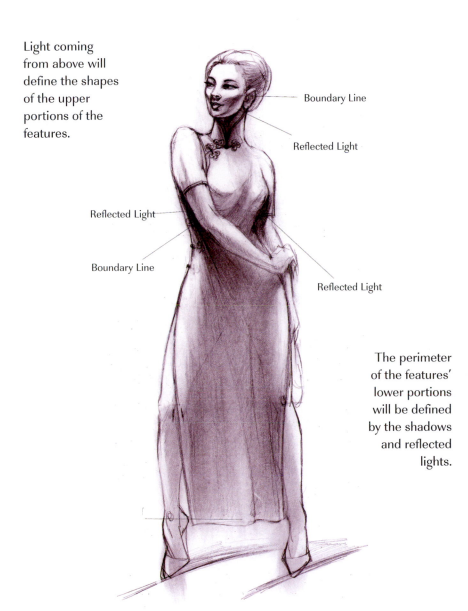

Boundary Line

Reflected Light

Reflected Light

Boundary Line

Reflected Light

The perimeter of the features' lower portions will be defined by the shadows and reflected lights.

6-2 Light from Below

Boundary Lines

Reflected Light

Reflected Light

When light comes from the bottom, the bottom of the features will be brighter.

A light source coming from either the left or right is easier for developing highlights and shadows. Because all features are clearly defined — such as the turning edge on the forehead, both sides of the nose bridge, and the edges of the cheekbone, jaw, chin, and other body parts — it works best simply to position shading on one side of the features. Light coming from the left or right is most common for costume designers (see Figures 6-3 and 6-4).

Whatever light source you choose, the shadows always fall along the natural forms of the body. Pronounced parts of the body will catch more highlights, and receding parts will stay in the shadows. The bottom planes and outer edges of body features most often show reflecting lights.

There are rules to learn, but that does not mean you must always follow them — you should know how to break them and how to let them work for you. In my costume figure drawings, most of the suggested light sources are from the upper front or the sides. Some of the drawings show mixed lighting sources. Cast shadows in the background or underneath the feet actually are used for setting off the figures rather than exhibiting natural-falling cast shadows. Use only necessary shadows, and do not overstress them.

Shadowing and highlighting accents body forms. Shading a shape in the back sets off shapes in the front; shading a shape at the side sets off shapes on the other side. Parts of a figure are not isolated; they are related together as a family. When drawing one part, compare it to the others. Keep the six elements of modeling highlights and shadows (highlight, light, boundary line, dark, reflected light, and cast shadow) in mind while drawing.

6-3 Light from Left

When the light is from the left side, the turning edges of the features are clearly defined.

Light and dark boundary lines

Reflected light

Reflected lights

Boundary lines

6-4 Light from Right

When the light comes from the right, all parts of the turning edges of the features are clearly defined.

Reflected light

Light and dark boundary lines

Reflected light

CHARACTERISTICS OF MATERIALS AND DRAWING STROKES

Different materials produce very different folds and wrinkles over the body. Utilizing different types of drawing and painting strokes to express textures and feelings of fabrics is the key to deciding material types. Theatrical costumes can be made from a tremendous variety of textures, colors, patterns, and weights of any types of materials. When drawing garments, try to communicate a sense of the particular material and the way it wrinkles, folds, and conforms to the body. Crisp and bold lines create hard-edged wrinkles and folds. Curved and linear lines create soft-edged wrinkles and folds. Deep shadowing will make the fabric look heavy. Prominent highlights are inherent on shiny fabrics.

Lines, shapes, and textures are closely related. Line strokes define direction at any given point — for instance, vertical and horizontal stripes on pants, or curly or straight hair. A group of scribbled lines can produce a rough and bulky texture. Textures can also be drawn entirely in linear lines without any shadows. Whether the image is done with linear lines, shadows, or scribbles, it plays a part in presenting the feeling, movement, and silhouette of the garment. Shiny materials reflect more light. Pile woven fabrics and wool materials absorb more light. A soft fabric flows and clings to the body and illustrates a soft silhouette. Crisp and bulky material has its own forms that tend to flare out from the body, especially when gathered. This creates a full silhouette.

Different materials are shown in individual ways:

🐚 **Stiff and bulky materials** usually show hard geometric creases and a full body silhouette. Drawing strokes should be firm, sharp, and bony to portray a crisp impression (see Figure 6-5).

🐚 **Soft, smooth, and flowing materials** are more capable of draping or hanging. They have a soft, clinging flare and follow body curves. Soft materials have fluid curves at the hem of the garments. Continuous, flowing, and linear lines and strokes should be used for drawing soft materials (see Figure 6-6).

🐚 **Rough-surfaced materials** have some kind of three-dimensional dynamic surface. Suggested textural strokes are composed of short broken lines, dots, shapes, or scribbled lines (see Figure 6-7).

🐚 **Shiny materials** contain high contrasts in value. The shiny surface of the material reflects highlights in broad areas. It can be soft or stiff. Use the same strokes you used for drawing soft materials as mentioned earlier for shiny materials. Use the same strokes you used for drawing stiff materials to draw stiff and shiny materials. Emphasize the contrast between light and dark (see Figure 6-8).

🐚 **Pile-woven materials,** such as velvet, velveteen, and velour, absorb light, drape, and are heavy. This type of fabric has a short, hairy surface. It produces soft-edged wrinkles and folds. Smearing strokes (with pencil media) can help to create this soft-edged, hairy look. Velvet material is effective when rendered in dark tones. To get a hairy look, use short strokes to contour the garment (see the cape in Figure 6-9).

🐚 **Fur** ranges in degrees of curvy and straight and can be long or short in length. It grows in different directions but always tapers to the ends. Tapered drawing strokes will achieve the furry look. Layer toning colored washes; then apply tapered strokes in the direction the fur grows. Keep the ends sharp (see Figures 6-10 through 6-12).

🐚 **Leather** can be suede or smooth. Suede has a dull surface compared to smooth leather. Suede causes the body to be more bulky, and the wrinkles and folds on the surface appear to have a rolling effect. Dry brush strokes are the best way to render suede materials. Sometimes choosing a rough-surfaced paper will help to effectively achieve the rough textured look. Using high contrast — very dark to very light — is the best way of expressing a smooth leather surface. Map highlights and shadows first, then carefully paint them. Keep a sharp, clean division between light and dark (see the shiny leather jacket in Figure 6-13).

6-5 Drawing Stiff and Bulky Material

TAFFETAS
UCF THEATRE DEPARTMENT SUMMER 1998

6-6 **Drawing Soft, Smooth, and Flowing Material**

6-7 **Drawing Rough-Surfaced Material**

6-8 Drawing Shiny Material

When drawing shiny material, emphasize the contrast between light and dark.

ESSIE ACT I

ESSIE ACT II

ESSIE ACT III

YOU CAN'T TAKE IT WITH YOU
UCF THEATRE
FALL 2000

C.D. - 960
COSTUME DESIGNER
SIGNATURE

6-9 **Drawing Pile-Woven Material**

GRAND DUCHESS
ACT III

GAY WELLINGTON
ACT II

Use tapered strokes
to draw a feather boa.

Pile woven material (the cape)
produces soft-edged wrinkles and
folds. Use short strokes to create
the hairy look.

YOU CAN'T TAKE IT WITY YOU
UCF THEATRE DEPARTMENT
FALL 2000

6-10   Drawing Fur

Tone the base color of the fur with wash first, then draw the fur with tapered strokes.

TAN HUAIXIANG
THE WALKER IN THE SNOW
FIFE / MICHAEL

6-11   Drawing Fur

TAN HUAIXIANG
THE WALKER IN THE SNOW
PIKOK

6-12   Drawing Fur

TAN HUAIXIANG
THE WALKER IN THE SNOW
SHAMAN

6-13   Drawing Leather

To create a smooth surface for leather, keep a sharp and clean division between light and dark.

PAINTING COSTUMES

There are two types of sketches to paint: a sketch with value and a sketch with no value but with outlines. The sketch with value (black and gray shadows created by pencil) is faster and easier to paint because value has already been indicated. You need to create value with colors if there is no value on the sketch.

Making copies of original sketches on a copy machine or scanning and printing transforms a sketch image onto lightweight paper for painting renderings. If you make a mistake or if the director doesn't like the colors you painted on the copy, you can make another copy of the original. Disadvantages are that copy machines and printers cannot process heavyweight paper, so you will have to paint on low quality paper—but it can be done.

Two basic ways of painting renderings are commonly used for either wet or dry media. One is painting from a light to a dark tone; and the other is painting from a dark to a light tone. The following vocabulary of colors will be used to explain the process of painting costume renderings: high-key color, low-key color, local color, and reflected color.

🌊 **High-key color** is any color that has a value level of middle gray or lighter. The color presents the light side of the garment directly hit by light.

🌊 **Low-key color** is any color that has a value level of middle gray or darker. The color presents a garment on the dark or poorly lighted side.

🌊 **Local color** is the color of the garment.

🌊 **Reflected color** is presented as reflected light, but in color. It can be a cool or warm tone, or it can be a complementary color of the garment.

The boundary color is darker than the garment's low-key color. Creating highlights and shadows develops value; color value is the relative degree of light or dark color. The six elements of creating highlights and shadows, discussed at the beginning of this chapter, can be applied to paint-colored renderings as well.

Watercolor media is used for demonstrating the process from light to dark. Watercolors are available in two main forms: pancakes and tubes. Pancake color is dry and needs to be moistened before use, whereas tube color is already moist and ready to use. Tube colors are more suitable for painting large-scaled drawings. Everyone has his or her own preferences.

In my opinion, watercolor is the fastest media for painting costume renderings. Watercolor is transparent, shows all toning layers, and is easily mixed and applied. Costume renderings are usually only small area projects, and sometimes only one or two strokes are needed for painting, especially when painting a sketch with value. Buy a color wheel and practice mixing colors. Keep in mind that adding less water to paint creates more high intensity color and deeper color values. Mixing complementary colors neutralizes colors. Mixing more than three colors together will produce muddy colors.

Painting from Light to Dark

Refer to Figures 6-14 through 6-16 for the following steps:

1. Use light pencil lines to map boundary lines between the light and dark sides.

2. Tone the light side only with the garment's high-key color. Leave some white areas on the paper (if it's white paper and if needed) as highlight spots on the garment. For a soft-edged effect, paint the next step while the paper is damp. For a hard-edged effect, wait until it's completely dry to start the next layer.

3. Add reflected color to the edges of the garment on the dark side. Spread the color toward the boundary line, but don't go over it. The value of the reflected color should be brighter than the shadow color but darker than the highlight.

4. Apply the local color of the garment on top of the high-key color. Don't color areas that are directly hit by light or where body forms are pronounced. Spread the paint to the dark side so it gradually merges with the reflected color.

5. Add shadows with the garment's low-key color only to the dark side of the garment. Start from the boundary line, and then merge with the reflected color.

6. Using the same local color mixed with the low-key color to paint the light side only where the light and dark meet to create a soft, gradual transition from the light side to the dark side.

7. Add details of highlights and very dark shadows (boundary line) to accent the rendering.

Figures 6-17 through 6-29 are design samples of watercolor rendering.

6-14 **Watercolor Rendering, Step One**

6-15A **Watercolor Rendering, Step Two (Dark to Light with Cool-Toned Shadow)**

6-15B Watercolor Rendering, Step Two (Light to Dark)

6-16 Watercolor Rendering, Step Three (Finished) — *Glengarry Glen Ross*

6-17 Design Sample of Watercolor Rendering —
Glengarry Glen Ross

6-18 Design Sample of Watercolor Rendering —
Glengarry Glen Ross

6-19 Design Sample of Watercolor Rendering —
Glengarry Glen Ross

6-20 Design Sample of Watercolor Rendering —
Glengarry Glen Ross

6-21 **Design Sample of Watercolor Rendering —** *Glengarry Glen Ross*

6-22 **Design Sample of Watercolor Rendering —** *Ceremonies in Dark Old Men*

6-23 Design Sample of Watercolor Rendering —
Cinderella

6-24 Design Sample of Watercolor Rendering —
Cinderella

6-25 Design Sample of Watercolor Rendering — *Cinderella*

6-26 Design Sample of Watercolor Rendering — *Cinderella*

6-27   Design Sample of Watercolor Rendering — *Cinderella*

6-28 Design Sample of Watercolor Rendering — *Cinderella*

6-29 Design Sample of Watercolor Rendering — *Cinderella*

Step-Sisters

CINDERELLA
Central Washington University
Theatre Arts Department

Rendering Sheer Material

Sheer material is transparent, revealing the body's contours. Sheer fabrics can be soft, flowing, and clinging to the body, or stiff and puffed away from the body. Use the same strokes (see Figures 6-6 and 6-9) as for painting soft-type material to render soft, flowing sheer material. Use the same strokes (see Figures 6-5 and 6-7) as for stiff material to render stiff and puffy sheer material.

To render sheer material (see Figures 6-30, 6-31, and 6-32), render the body first with skin-tone paint. Then paint the garment. The contours or outlines of the garment are fine and continuous lines. For stiff fabric types, contour lines should be crisp.

6-30 Rendering Sheer Material with Watercolor Medium — Step One

6-31 Rendering Sheer Material with Watercolor Medium — Step Two

6-32 Rendering Sheer Material with Watercolor Medium — Step Three (Finished)

Painting from Dark to Light

An acrylic medium is used for the following demonstration (see Figures 6-33, 6-34, and 6-35). Watercolor techniques can be used with acrylic paints (I work from dark to light with both watercolors and acrylics). Acrylics are water-soluble when wet. Once dry, they are waterproof; you can paint over acrylics without lifting the color beneath. The dry color tone is the same as when it was wet. These paints can be used opaquely (thick build-up, like oil paints) or transparently in a thin layer by mixing in water. Acrylics dry fast so you have to work fast. Create highlight colors by adding more water to watercolor paint and vice versa for creating darker paint. With acrylics, this can be done in two ways: add water to dilute the paint, or mix in white or other high value paints to develop lighter-toned highlight colors. Mix in black, grays, or complementary colors to produce dark colors and shadows. Don't mix colors too thoroughly, and avoid mixing more than three colors together because it will make the paint look muddy and reduce the freshness.

1. Use light pencil lines to map boundary lines between the light and dark sides.

2. Paint the entire shadow side with reflected color. As mentioned before, reflected color can be in cool or warm tones or a complimentary color of the garment. Reflected color value is brighter than the shadow color but darker than the highlight color.

3. Tone the entire light side of the garment with high-key color, and leave some white areas as highlight spots.

4. For acrylics, use a wash technique (used also in watercolors) for a transparent effect. Apply local color (thin paint with water only) on top of high-key color (leave areas where light directly hits) on the shadow side and merge with reflected color. When local color overlaps the reflected color beneath, it automatically creates shadow colors.

5. For an opaque look, mix selected paint with white or high-value colors to brighten high-key colors. Mix with black, gray, or complementary colors to darken or neutralize local or low-key colors. Apply local color to the light side and paint around highlight areas. Apply low-key color from the boundary line in the dark side, and then merge with reflected color.

6. Mix the same local color with the same low-key color, and paint the light side in areas where light and dark meet to create a smooth progressive shift from light to dark. The value of the mixed color should be darker than the local color and lighter than the low-key color.

7. Add highlights and very dark shadows (the boundary line) to accent the rendering.

6-33 Acrylic Rendering — Step One

6-34 Acrylic Rendering — Step Two

6-35 Acrylic Rendering—Step Three (Finished)

Painting from dark to light and vice versa should work the same if the painting is under control. Painting on a dry surface will create hard, crisp edges. Painting on a damp surface will create a soft-edged look. Working at a fast speed helps in developing soft edges well.

Gouache colors are intense and opaque. Gouaches are similar to acrylics because both can be mixed together and thinned with water. Mix them with white paint to create opaque tints and thin with water for transparent colors. They can be used to paint from light to dark or vice versa. The difference between acrylics and gouaches are that acrylics dry fast and become waterproof once dry. Gouaches dry more slowly, which allows more time for work. On the other hand, gouaches have a tendency to bleed through if one coat of paint is on top of another coat. Acrylics stay the same tone when dry, whereas gouache dries to a lighter tone. Easy ways to control gouache paints include mixing the paint one shade darker than the actual color being created and avoiding back-and-forth strokes when painting on top of another layer.

Background color can be painted before or after rendering the sketch. Painting the background first is the safe way because any mistakes can ruin a painted rendering.

Figures 6-36 through 6-42 are design samples of acrylic rendering.

6-36 **Design Sample of Acrylic Rendering**—*Misalliance*

6-37 **Design Sample of Acrylic Rendering**—*Misalliance*

6-38 Design Sample of Acrylic Rendering—*Steel City*

6-39 Design Sample of Acrylic Rendering—*Romeo & Juliet*

ROMEO & JULIET
CWU Theatre Arts Department

Romeo

Juliet

Juliet

6-40 Design Sample of Acrylic Rendering—*Romeo & Juliet*

Guests

ROMEO & JULIET
CENTRAL WASHINGTON UNIVERSITY
THEATRE ARTS DEPARTMENT

6-41 Design Sample of Acrylic Rendering—*Romeo & Juliet*

ROMEO & JULIET
CWU THEATRE ARTS DEPARTMENT

Nurse

6-42 Design Sample of Acrylic Rendering—*The Butterfingers Angel*

THE BUTTERFINGERS ANGEL
UCF Theatre Department
fall 1998

Painting with Markers

There are many different types of markers available on the market. Staedtler-Mars Graphic 3000 and Pantone markers are my favorites. Markers are convenient for quick renderings and are an extremely useful media for costume design. Colors range widely in intensity and permanence. Markers let you create detailed drawings in little time. They can be mixed by overlapping colors or with a blender pen and can be combined with other media. Be careful when buying markers, and try them first before purchasing. Try not to buy the primary/pure or bright-color markers; they are too strong and difficult to mix. They tend to look garish and provide a less realistic impression. It is hard to create an illusion of space between you and the object. If you paint a garment just "red" without mixing any other colors together, your figure will look "cartoony" and unrealistic.

EXAMPLES

- Finish sketches to be ready for coloring (see Figure 6-43A).

- Tone a garment with one color marker to create value by overlapping. This gives a smooth surface and a soft-edged look (see example 1 in Figure 6-43B).

- Overlap complementary colors to create value by applying them at the shadow areas and then coloring over it. This creates a light to dark contrast (see example 2 in Figure 6-43B).

- Overlap with gray tones to achieve value. How many layers of gray to paint and how dark the gray should be are based on the local color of the garment. The gray color can be painted before or after painting local color. Experiment mixing with grays before painting (see example 3 in Figure 6-43B).

- Tone the garment with markers (finished, see figure 6-43C).

- Create details with gel pens. Fine-point gel pens are available in sparkle or nonsparkle colors. There are also Super Vibrant opaque-colored pens that appear clearly on dark surfaces, and they can be used to draw patterns and lines. They are the best tool for adding details (see Figures 6-44, 6-45, and 6-46).

Figures 6-47 through 6-49 are design samples of painting with markers.

6-43 A Toning the Garment with Markers, Step One (Finished Sketches)

TAFFETAS
UCF THEATRE DEPARTMENT SUMMER 1998

6-43 B   **Toning the Garment with Markers, Step Two**

Example 1   Example 2   Example 3   (same as Example 2)

TAFFETAS
UCF THEATRE DEPARTMENT SUMMER 1998

6-43 C   Toning the Garment with Markers (Finished)

Example 1   Example 2   Example 3   (same as Example 2)

TAFFETAS
UCF THEATRE DEPARTMENT SUMMER 1998

C.D. - 960
COSTUME DESIGNER
SIGNATURE

6-44 Creating Details with Gel Pens, Step One: Finish Sketch

6-45 Creating Details with Gel Pens, Step Two: Toning the Entire Garment

6-46 Creating Details with Gel Pens, Step Three: Adding Details/ Patterns/Designs to Garment

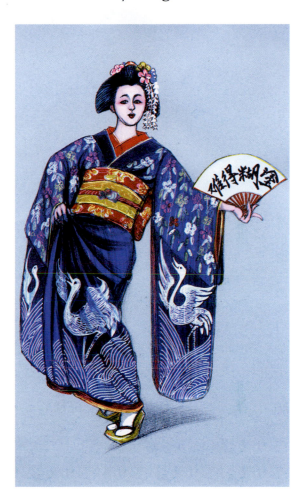

6-47 **Design Sample of Painting with Markers**—*Big River*

6-48 **Design Sample of Painting with Markers—*Big River***

BIG RIVER
UCF THEATRE DEPARTMENT
SPRING 1999

C.D. - 960
COSTUME DESIGNER

6-49 Design Sample of Painting with Markers—*Big River*

Creating Texture

Creating a textured garment can be done by painting with layers of colors and strokes to add the illusion of roughness to the surface of the paper. In this section, I am going to discuss how to use colored pencils to create textured garments. Colored pencils are clean, quick, and portable. They are very useful for quick sketches, are simple to apply, and allow plenty of time to make adjustments while drawing. They can be blended, mixed, and built up in multiple layers. They can produce translucent and opaque effects.

There are two kinds of colored pencils you may want to have for drawing costumes: Prisma and water-soluble colored pencils. Prisma colored pencils are strong, light, and fast, and provide rich and vivid colors. A set of Prisma colored pencils lasts for many years. Water-soluble colored pencils have all the advantages of Prisma colored pencils in addition to being water soluble. Adding water creates watercolor effects, and can create a transparent look with texture. After coloring with colored pencil, add water to dissolve it but do not dissolve all the color evenly for a textured look. Water-soluble pencils are easier to handle than watercolor pigments. Both Prisma colored pencils and water-soluble colored pencils can be used in combination with other media to create special effects.

CREATING A PINSTRIPED SUIT AND PLAID DRESS

Creating stripes and textures using indentation marks is very effective (see Figure 6-50). The indentations build up another layer of dimension on the drawing paper. I discovered this by trying to remove indentation marks from my drawings. Then I found that they are useful for creating textures of costumes. This method works well with dry media, but it doesn't work with wet media because wet paint bleeds into the indentation marks and flattens the image.

- Place sketching paper on a surface softer than a drawing table (on top of a paperback book), and make striped indentation marks with a butter knife (or another dull object) on the sketch of the garment before coloring. This creates white stripes on the garment, and a soft surface allows deeper indentation marks to be etched.

- When coloring the sketch, move the paper to a hard surface for better results because a hard surface will protect indentation marks. Hold the colored pencil at a 35 degree or less angle while coloring to avoid pigments getting into the indentation marks.

- Color highlights of the pants first.

- Color reflected color second.

- Color the sketch with the garment's local color and merge it with both highlights and reflected colors.

- Add shadows (the boundary line is the darkest in the shadow area) and merge the shadow color with reflected light.

CREATING ROUGH-TEXTURE FABRICS

Creating other types of rough-texture fabrics, such as horizontal stripes, plaids, and twill, woven, or irregular patterns can be achieved using the same indentation mark procedure (see Figure 6-51). Paint or color in a 35 degree or less angle to your pattern. For example, if you etch vertical stripes on a suit, color with horizontal movements. Make sure you color quickly so you don't color in your indentation marks. If making a plaid pattern, color diagonally. The point is, try to color in a different direction from your indentation marks.

For color or multiple-color textures, simply apply one or more layers of the desired foundation colors (use watercolors, or markers for a solid, smooth surface) and wait until the paper completely dries; then make indentation marks. Choose a contrasting set of multiple colors. The greater the contrast, the better the outcome. Thick, heavy drawing paper is best for creating this type of textured drawing because deeper indentations are possible and the pressure is strongly supported.

Figures 6-52 through 6-60 are design samples of textured costumes.

6-50 **Creating Stripes and Plaids with Indentation Marks**

6-51 **Creating Twill, Woven, or Irregular Patterns with Indentation Marks (Colored Pencils and Markers)**

6-52 Design Sample of Textured Costumes—
Tom Sawyer

6-53 Design Sample of Textured Costumes—*Tintypes*

6-54 **Design Sample of Textured Costumes—** *The Mystery of Irma Vep*

6-55 **Design Sample of Textured Costumes—*The Mystery of Irma Vep***

6-56 Design Sample of Textured Costumes — *The Mystery of Irma Vep*

6-57 Design Sample of Textured Costumes—
Ceremonies in Dark Men

6-58 Design Sample of Textured Costumes—
The Lion in Winter

6-59 Design Sample of Textured Costumes — *The Lion in Winter*

6-60 Design Sample of Textured Costumes — *The Taming of the Shrew*

THE LION IN WINTER
JOHN

Grumio

Curtis

THE TAMING OF THE SHREW
DEPARTMENT OF THEATRE ARTS
UTAH STATE UNIVERSITY

PAINTING THE HEAD AND FACE

Facial expression is a main focus for my character costume figure drawings. I usually keep the face lightly and simply painted with a suggested flesh tone and shadows. You can use any media to render the head and face. For a transparent effect, mix paint with water. For an opaque effect, mix white into the paint. Flesh-toned markers or colored pencils also are used often. I like to use watercolors because I am able to invent any color I want.

Two examples of painting heads and faces follow. They can be painted either from dark to light (Figure 6-61) or from light to dark (Figure 6-62). Common shadows that appear on the face are at the eye sockets, sides and bottom of the nose, cheekbone areas, upper lips, temple area, under the jawline, and bottom of the lip.

Using opaque colors. Add a little white to the skin-tone color. Lighter skin has a pinkish glow. A dark skin tone shows a tan or is brownish in color. Apply the desired skin tone to the entire face (don't paint the inside of the eyes). Add red to create rouge color. Add dark colors to create shadows, and apply it to shady areas. Color the cheek areas before the first layer of paint dries, for a soft look. Create cheek colors by tinting the skin tone with red shades. Keep the top eyelid thicker and darker than the bottom one. Iris color can be based on the character. Keep the top lip slightly darker than the bottom lip. The hairline and eyebrows are soft-edged for a realistic look. Tone the entire hair growth area with a wet-wash of hair-foundation color and leave white areas as highlights. Then add dark colors to the hair-foundation color, to create a shadow area. After the foundation and shadow colors dry completely, apply curved strokes with a fine brush for texture. Accent dark colors at the boundary line for contrast.

Using transparent colors. Use transparent colors to paint the head and face. Mix paint with water to create a skin-tone color and apply it to the entire face, but leave some highlight areas such as the eyesockets, nose bridge, upper cheekbones, and the top of the chin. Add shadow colors to shadow areas as mentioned previously. Reflected colors should be applied at the feature's bottom portions for a three-dimensional form. Paint the hair using the previous technique.

6-61 Painting from Dark to Light

Step One

Step Two

Step Three

6-62 Painting from Light to Dark

Step One

Step Two

Step Three

A good rendering is one that is accurate in its proportions with exciting movement, balance, facial expression, and clothing that works and fits with the body. State the garment well; apply dynamic use of space; add visible pencil strokes to increase dimension to the fabric; use vigorous lines to accent and add swing to the figure; and accent colors for a harmonious and well-contrasted color equilibrium. Create your own imaginative and unique images.

DECORATING THE BACKGROUND OF THE COSTUME DESIGN

A background supports and enhances a design but should not take away from the design. The background can be painted in color or can include shadows and shapes. It can be illustrated with objects such as furniture or scenery. Frames or particular lines may be used as well. A background creates an environment that sets off the figure and the costumes. Consider proper background decoration as part of the design concept; it enhances and enriches the three-dimensional effect of the whole body. When choosing a background, try to create a mood that fits the play and the character rather than just painting any random color. Keep the background style of the design consistent throughout each drawing to unify the design themes. Using complementary colors is recommended; I often choose black or gray colors because those tones can easily be harmonized and blended with other colors.

Shading underneath a figure's feet exists in most of my designs. I choose to do so because it is simple, fast, and easy to control, yet provides dimension and space. It also provides a location or horizon for the figure to stand on. Some shadows in the background behind figures are not necessarily logically positioned but, rather, are decorations. Even cast shadows added underneath feet do not exactly reflect the direction from which the light is coming, and may not match the shadows on the garments. They are just decorations that provide contrast.

Creating a type background for a figure is a personal choice. You may develop a uniquely styled background or choose to do no background at all. Obviously, decorating the background should not be the main focus for costume-design renderings. Costumes and character figures are the central concentration. Background decoration is always just a complementary element. Adding a busy background is like drawing legs on a snake—it is uncalled-for and may ruin the design.

If you choose to add a background design, remember these two words, "contrast and decorate." Contrast value, size, color, texture, and details. Decorate the elements you put on the background in a supportive and harmonious manner that won't take away from your costumes.

Figures 6-63 through 6-76 are design samples of creating background.

6-63 Design Sample of Creating Background —
Cross-Hatching with Pencil

6-64 Design Sample of Creating Background —
Cross-Hatching with Pencil

AFTER THE FALL
MAGGIE

AFTER THE FALL
MOTHER

6-65 Design Sample of Creating Background—
With Textured Paper

6-66 Design Sample of Creating Background—
With Textured Paper

6-67   **Design Sample of Creating Background—
With Textured Paper**

6-68 Design Sample of Creating Background—With Tinted Paper

6-69 **Design Sample of Creating Background—With Decorative Paper**

6-70 **Design Sample of Creating Background—With Decorative Paper**

6-71 Design Sample of Creating Background—With Decorative Paper

6-72 Design Sample of Creating Background—
With Tinted Paper and Framed

THE FROG PRINCE
Frog /Prince

6-73 Design Sample of Creating Background—
With Tinted Paper and Framed

THE FROG PRINCE
Palace Guard

6-74 **Design Sample of Creating Background—Adding an Object behind the Characters**

6-75 **Design Sample of Creating Background—With Tinted Paper and a Circular Composition**

6-76   Design Sample of Creating Background — Creating an Environment for Characters

DRAWING SUPPLIES

A wide array of paper, paints, brushes, and pencils are available on the market. Better quality supplies will obviously produce higher quality renderings. High-quality materials can visually help poor quality drawings. However, use low-quality materials to practice your sketching skills, such as achieving correct proportion and balance, creating body movements, capturing facial expressions, creating highlights and shadows, and using strokes to create textures. Exercise these skills with economical materials, but do your final project with high-quality materials.

I experiment with all types of paper, especially ones with texture. Throughout my design samples in this book, you will notice that the sketches and renderings are done on many different kinds of paper. Some renderings are painted with a combination of media.

As a costume designer, you should have these major drawing tools in hand:

❧ **Pencils.** A mechanical pencil with a replaceable eraser is best for making costume character drawings. Leads for mechanical pencils include HB, B, and 2B. 2B-lead is commonly used. Mechanical leads can make linear lines, hatching or crosshatching lines for shading, and overlapping lines for thick contour lines. Hard leads make grays, and soft leads make blacks. You don't have to sharpen the pencil while drawing. Graphite drawing pencils are useful for class work and large still-life drawings. Their leads range from 9H to H, and HB to 9B. H-type pencils are hard and good for time-consuming projects, and can produce broad sidestrokes. Hard pencils also can be used during the beginning stages of drawing and mapping light marks or outlines of highlights and shadows. Soft leads are efficient for creating value.

❧ **Charcoal pencils.** They are truly black graphite pencils and can produce firm, fluid, bold, and vigorous lines. Smudging will produce high-contrast rich tonal effects. They are good for class drawing projects. Charcoal drawings need to be sprayed with fixative to protect the surface of the drawing.

❧ **Brushes.** Natural-hair brushes (sable bristles are the best) hold paint well for watercolor paintings. Synthetic-fiber brushes are slightly stiffer than natural-hair brushes and are good for acrylics and gouache paints. Brushes come in small and large, round and flat shapes. You should own both types of brushes in different sizes. A larger rendering requires a bigger brush for an even and smooth look.

❧ **Paper.** There are many different drawing and painting papers to choose from. To choose the correct one, experiment with them yourself to figure out what is most suitable for your renderings.

In general, watercolors go on watercolor paper. There is heavy or lightweight paper; I use lightweight paper because it can go through a copy machine (I paint on copies). I like watercolor pad, acid free, cold press, 90 lb. paper. It comes in different sizes, 11 × 15 or 9 × 12. Sometimes my renderings are done on copy paper. If you like heavier watercolor paper, you either can draw the sketch directly on painting paper or trace the image onto heavy painting paper.

Bristol paper is good quality drawing paper preferred by a lot of costume designers because it is made from natural fibers. It can go through some copy machines (sometimes by luck). Bristol paper is ideal for dry media and light washes.

Sketchpads are made for all purposes and are similar to Bristol paper, but thinner.

Ink jet paper has an ultra smooth surface, and is very good for markers, colored pencils, light-wash watercolors, or acrylics. It is easy to make copies by copy machine or printer.

Illustration boards are good for both watercolor and acrylic paints. For an even wash, damp the surface of the paper before painting. Illustration boards are available in a wide range of colors. If you need a contrasting background, choose a tinted board.

Tinted paper sells in sheets in a variety of colors. Choose the appropriate color for your rendering. Deep-tinted paper is good for contrast, but not suitable for watercolors and markers (the tinted color will show through transparent paint). It works for other media such as acrylics, gouaches, and colored pencils.

❧ **Paints.** Watercolors, acrylics, and gouaches, as mentioned earlier, are my recommendations. A color-mixing palette and a drawing board will be needed for painting renderings.

❧ **Artist Tape.** This is needed for taping down the corners or the edges of the paper, in order to keep it flat when it dries.

Any material will work for you if you know how to draw. A pocket sketchbook is a good way to practice quick sketches. Draw as much as you can on different materials, even on brown pattern paper.

7

Costume Rendering Gallery

7-1 A Costume Design for *Death of a Salesman*

7-1 B Costume Design for *Death of a Salesman*

7-1 C Costume Design for *Death of a Salesman*

DEATH OF A SALESMAN
UCF THEATRE SPRING 2002

BERNARD
AS YOUNG
ACT I

BERNARD
AS YOUNG
ACT II

C.D. - 960
COSTUME DESIGNER
SIGNATURE

7-1 D Costume Design for *Death of a Salesman*

DEATH OF A SALESMAN
UCF THEATRE SPRING 2002

BEN
ACT I & II

C.D. - 960
COSTUME DESIGNER
SIGNATURE

7-1 E Costume Design for *Death of a Salesman*

7-1 F Costume Design for *Death of a Salesman*

7-1 G Costume Design for *Death of a Salesman*

7-1 H Costume Design for *Death of a Salesman*

7-1 I Costume Design for *Death of a Salesman*

DEATH OF A SALESMAN
U.C.F. THEATRE SPRING 2002

HAPPY
ACT I

HAPPY
ACT II

HAPPY
ACT II

7-1 J Costume Design for *Death of a Salesman*

DEATH OF A SALESMAN
U.C.F. THEATR SPRING 2002

HAPPY
AS YOUNG
ACT I

HAPPY
AS YOUNG
ACT II

7-1 K Costume Design for *Death of a Salesman*

7-1 L Costume Design for *Death of a Salesman*

7-2 A   Costume Design for *Anything Goes*

Act II-1, 2 & 4

Act II-5

ANYTHING GOES
Billy Crocker
UCF Theatre Spring/2000

7-2 B Costume Design for *Anything Goes*

Act I-3

Act I-3

Act I-8

Act II-1 & 2

Act II-5

Act I-1

Act I-8

Act II-1 & 2

ANYTHING GOES
Erma
UCF Theatre Spring/2000

7-2 C Costume Design for *Anything Goes*

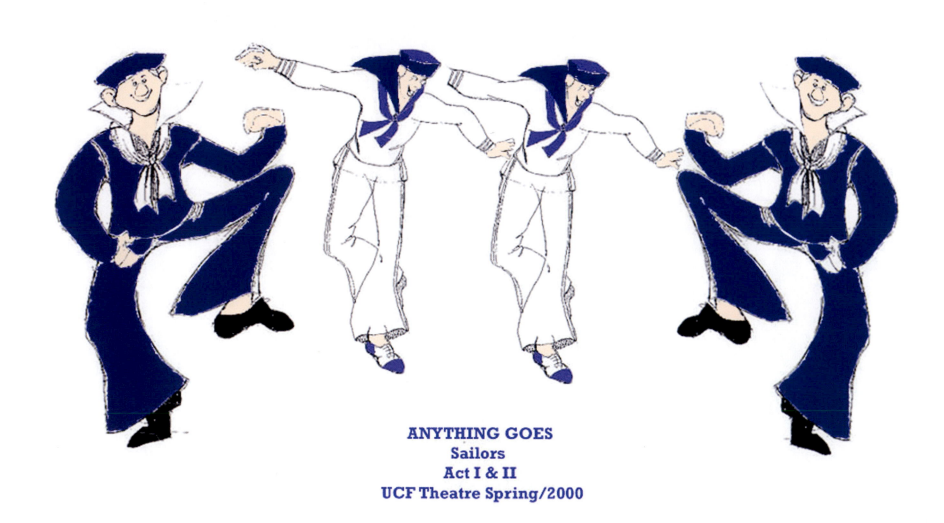

ANYTHING GOES
Sailors
Act I & II
UCF Theatre Spring/2000

7-3 A Costume Design for *Look Homeward, Angel*

7-3 B Costume Design for *Look Homeward, Angel*

LOOK HOMEWARD, ANGEL
UCF DEPARTMENT OF THEATRE
SPRING 2002

7-3 C Costume Design for *Look Homeward, Angel*

7-3 D Costume Design for *Look Homeward, Angel*

7-3 E Costume Design for *Look Homeward, Angel*

Will
Act I & II

Will
Act II

LOOK HOMEWARD, ANGEL
UCF DEPARTMENT OF THEATRE
SPRING 2002

Jack Clatt
Act I & III

Jack Clatt
Act II

LOOK HOMEWARD, ANGEL
UCF DEPARTMENT OF THEATRE
SPRING 2002

7-3 F Costume Design for *Look Homeward, Angel*   **7-3 G** Costume Design for *Look Homeward, Angel*

Mr. Farrel
Act I & III

Mr. Farrel
Act II

Mrs. Snowden
Act I & III

Mrs. Snowden
Act II

LOOK HOMEWARD, ANGEL
UCF DEPARTMENT OF THEATRE
SPRING 2002

LOOK HOMEWARD, ANGEL
UCF DEPARTMENT OF THEATRE
Spring 2002

7-3 H Costume Design for *Look Homeward, Angel*

Mrs. Clatt
Act I & III

Mrs. Clatt
Act II

LOOK HOMEWARD, ANGEL
UCF DEPARTMENT OF THEATRE
SPRING 2002

7-4 A Costume Design for *Amadeus*

7-4 B Costume Design for *Amadeus*

7-4 C Costume Design for *Amadeus*

7-4 D Costume Design for *Amadeus*

7-4 E Costume Design for *Amadeus*

CONSTANZE

AMADEUS
UCF THEATRE DEPT.

7-4 F   **Costume Design for** *Amadeus*

7-4 G Costume Design for *Amadeus*

7-4 H Costume Design for *Amadeus*

7-41 Costume Design for *Amadeus*

7-4 J Costume Design for *Amadeus*

7-4 K Costume Design for *Amadeus*

7-5 A Costume Design for *No Place to Be Somebody*

7-5 B Costume Design for *No Place to Be Somebody*

7-5 C Costume Design for *No Place to Be Somebody*

7-6 A Costume Design for *Dracula*

Lacy

DRACULA
Central Washington University
Theatre Arts Department

7-6 B Costume Design for *Dracula*

Mina

DRACULA
Central Washington University
Theatre Arts Department

7-6 C Costume Design for *Dracula*

DRACULA Quincy
Central Washington University
Theatre Arts Department

Jonathan

7-6 D Costume Design for *Dracula*

Catherine

Townsman

Townswoman

Arthur

Albertina

DRACULA
Central Washington University
Theatre Atrs Department

7-6 E Costume Design for *Dracula*

Van Helsing

Elizabeth S. DRACULA
Central Washington University
Theatre Arts Department

7-7 A Costume Design for *13 Rue de L'Amour*

7-7 B Costume Design for *13 Rue de L'Amour*

7-7 C Costume Design for *13 Rue de L'Amour*

7-7 D Costume Design for *13 Rue de L'Amour*

Leontine

Moricet

ACT II

13 RUE DE L'AMOUR
Central Washington University
Theatre Arts Department

13 RUD DE L'AMOUR
Central Washington University
Theatre Arts Department

Duchotel

7-7 E Costume Design for *13 Rue de L'Amour*

7-8 A Costume Design for *Tom Sawyer*

7-8 B Costume Design for *Tom Sawyer*

7-8 C Costume Design for *Tom Sawyer*

7-9 A Costume Design for *Elves and Shoemaker*

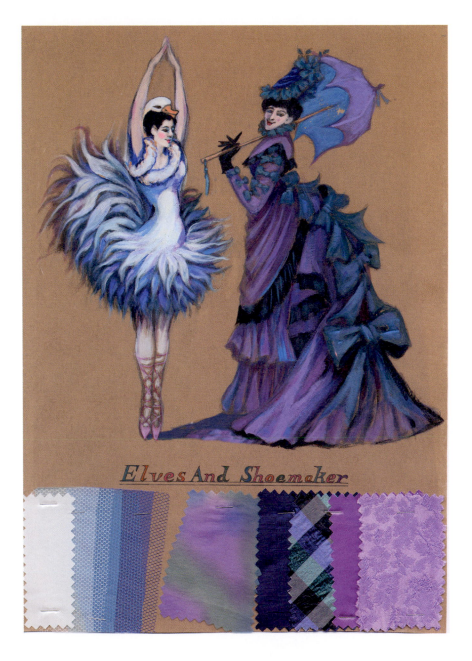

7-9 B Costume Design for *Elves and Shoemaker*

7-9 C Costume Design for *Elves and Shoemaker*

Elves And Shoemaker

7-10   Graduate Assignment: Set Design for *Homecoming*

Graduate Assignment: SET DESIGN for HOMECOMING, by Tan Huaixiang

7-11 Graduate Assignment: Set Design for *Homecoming*

Graduate Assignment: SET DESIGN for HOMECOMING, by Tan Huaixiang

7-12 Computer Auto-CAD

COMPUTER AUTO-CAD
Designed by Tan Huaixiang
Fall 1990

7-13 Computer Auto-CAD

COMPUTER AUTO-CAD
Designed by Tan Huaixiang
Fall 1990

7-14 Computer Applications

TXA 635   Spring 1991--Special Topics-Computer Applications
Cornell University

12th International Trade Show and Conference for Event and Media Engineering

01-03 June 2005

Join the expert world of stage technology

Berlin Exhibition Centre

www.showtech.de

Organiser:

 Messe Berlin Reed

Tel: +49(0)211/ 90 191 -240
Fax: +49(0)211/ 90 191 -244
info@showtech.de

Sponsor: